Seasons

and

Celebrations

Prayers for Christian Worship
Book 1

Seasons
and
Celebrations

Compiled by
Donald Hilton

NCEC

Other books by Donald Hilton

Celebrating Series
Risks of Faith
Raw materials of Faith
Results of Faith
After Much Discussion

Compiled by Donald Hilton

Prayers for the Church Community
(with Roy Chapman)
Liturgy of Life
Flowing Streams

Cover design: Peggy Chapman

Published by:
National Christian Education Council
1020 Bristol Road
Selly Oak
Birmingham
B29 6LB

British Library Cataloguing in Publication Data:
A catalogue record for this book is available from the British Library.

ISBN 0 - 7197 - 0887 - 7

First published 1996

Typeset by National Christian Education Council
Printed by Ebenezer Baylis & Son Ltd

Contents

Seasons and Celebrations is a collection of prayers written by an ecumenical group of writers. As ministers in local churches, most of the authors lead worship regularly, so the majority of prayers have already been used in the worship of a local congregation. Almost all are original prayers and are previously unpublished.

The first part of *Seasons and Celebrations* offers prayers for the Sundays of the Christian Year. The second part focuses on Sundays of international importance such as the Week of Prayer for Christian Unity; Sundays of national importance including Remembrance Sunday; and local celebrations, particularly the Church Anniversary.

Although I have sought to give coherence to the whole collection, the individual style of each of the contributors has been retained. It is hoped that the resulting variety will make the prayers useful in a large number of situations.

In each section of the collection, the prayers are offered in the following liturgical order: Invocation, Adoration, Confession, Thanksgiving, Supplication, Intercession and Commitment. Those parts of the prayers which are printed in bold type can be used as a congregational response. Most biblical quotations are from the Revised English Bible.

Although written primarily for ministers and local preachers, for whom the leading of worship is a regular responsibility, the authors also believe that the book will be helpful for those who lead worship in women's meetings, youth meetings, Bible study groups, etc. and as an aid to private devotion.

This collection is offered in the hope that it will enrich the worship of the people of God as they meet to praise the God and Father of our Lord Jesus Christ.

Donald Hilton
Leeds
1996

No matter how imaginative and resourceful a person might be, there will be something in *Seasons and Celebrations* to bring new joy and delight. As I read them prayerfully, there arose in me three responses. Some of the words call forth a glad recognition of familiarity; here are thoughts I have had and expressed in similar ways and it is good to have that affirmation. Here also are prayers that I come to with a willingness to own what is said in a way so much more succinct and evocative than I could have expressed it, and which make me nod my head as I read and receive this widening of my prayer vocabulary. There are some however for which I shall always be grateful, for these are the thoughts that I could not have had unless another had expressed them. These come as a kind of revelation from someone else's thought pattern and prayer experience in a way which widens my understanding and deepens my appreciation of the differences which enrich our perception of God.

I do want to commend this collection of prayers written by many people, all of whom pray deeply themselves and have experience of leading others in prayer. The prayers are designed both to be used as they are and to be taken as a resource for the preparation of other prayers. This volume covers seasons of the Christian year and offers prayers for special celebrations.

Those who are familiar with other works which Donald Hilton has written or edited will be grateful for yet another tool in their workshop. Those for whom it is a new experience are in for a real treat.

Revd Dr Kathleen Richardson OBE
Moderator of the Free Church Federal Council

Part 1
The Christian Year

Advent

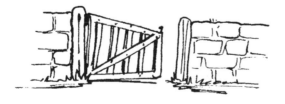

1 Gracious God,
coming to your people in a child,
bringing to your people new hope,
gifting to your people new life,
    we come before you in worship,
    we bring before you all we are,
    we lay before you our gift of praise.
Have us know your nearness,
make us feel your presence,
show us now your will,
    for we too would come,
    and bring
    and gift
    in the name and for the sake of our coming Lord Jesus Christ.

2 God of light,
shining strongly,
focused on the deep darkness of despair,
flooding the inky blackness of isolation,
blazing bright on the dark night of sin,
piercing the shade of the pains of injustice,
bathing the world with a sun of renewal,
we eagerly wait for the coming of Jesus
as a dawn of healing and of hope and of judgement.
    Lord, let the light of your presence burst in on our worship,
    making our ordinary offering burn with the brilliance of your
        Spirit's inspiration.
    In the name of the Light of the World we pray.

3 Coming God,
    coming in our Lord Jesus,
    coming for outcasts,
    coming to confound the proud,
    coming to surprise with joy the sad.
Come amongst us now
in the power and presence of your Spirit,
as we come into your presence in praise.
In the name and for the sake of Jesus Christ.

4

Advent God,
we meet as your people.
At times the world seems dark,
cold and lonely.
We meet confident that your love
is working to bring warmth and light.
Be with us,
Immanuel; the God who comes close.

5

Advent God,
we meet to be inspired by your promised coming,
to learn your will
    through people who speak out for justice,
to see your power
    in people who bring light to others,
to find your truth
    from people who point to your light.
Be with us,
Immanuel; the God who comes close.

6

Advent God,
we meet preparing to greet you.
Turn us around to find your way.
Guide us into a lifestyle appropriate to your coming kingdom,
so that we may prepare the way for others
and lead them in the path of peace.
Be with us,
Immanuel; the God who comes close.

7

Advent God,
we come responding to your call.
You used the most unlikely people
in the preparation for your kingdom.
A peasant girl became the mother of our Lord,
and a simple family nurtured him.
Encourage us as we remember the obedience of others.
Be with us,
Immanuel; the God who comes close.

8 ✓ God and Father of our coming Lord Jesus Christ, the time of Christ's Advent draws near and we feel a mixture of excitement and apprehension. Excitement for the hope he heralds; apprehension for the judgement he brings. This yearly round brings pain as well as pleasure.

We are innkeepers, for our hearts are too ready to cry: 'No room here!' and yet we want to be the shepherds who heard the angels, and gathered in wonder and in praise at the cradle.

We are Herods, fearful for our position, and yet we want to be the Wise Men who bowed and gave gifts.

We ache to welcome the Christ-child, and yet we agonize at the cost of commitment.

Living God, fill us with wonder and keen anticipation for the glory to be revealed. Take from us unfitting fear and give us an expectation of renewal. Speak to us of your enduring nearness as we draw near to you in worship.

9 Gracious God,
as the days shorten
and the pale, wintry sun
bathes the sky with light,
so may our anxiety abate
and the warmth of your love
cleanse and purify our lives.
Promised One,
as the ice skims the pond
and bright frost
gilds the leaf with glory,
may the clarity of your call
awaken us to new hope
and new beginnings.
Holy Spirit of transformation,
help us to clear the way
for the coming Christ-child.
As the red sun sinks behind black branches,
slip into our lives,
and surprise us by the welcome warmth
of your coming.

Candle Prayers
Prayers for the lighting of Advent candles

10

The flickering flames
of the Advent crown
dance dangerously:
giving warmth and light,
consuming wick and wax.
And in their shape we can sometimes see
a cross described.
> Loving Lord Jesus,
> the cradle and the cross dovetail:
> the birth of hope, the sacrifice of love.
> You were born for our sake:
> the presents of the Magi were a kingly crown.
>> You were consumed for our sake:
>> an altogether different crown
>> of piercing thorns,
>> pressed hard into your flesh,
>> drawing blood and tears.

11

Each candle on the Christmas crown of Advent expectation
kindles a hope within us;
and each grows less by burning,
recalling the cost you bore.
Lord of Cradle and Cross,
we light our candles in thanksgiving,
we gather in worship,
and we wait in wonder.

12   Loving God,
          alive for us like dancing flames of Advent candles:
              drawing us near to your light,
              burning away the darkness of misdeeds,
              and firing our lives with your purpose,
          make us living flames of passion and commitment:
              exposed to the winds of the world's ways,
              unquenched by their swirling despair,
              and ever four-square in our commitment to Christ.

13   The candle flames of Advent,
          flickering in the draughts,
          dance welcome and warmth.
          How right to see them that way.
              How wrong if we are so sealed from the world
              that all is still and the flames stand straight and strong.
          How right to see the light of the life of Christ
          bright and yet vulnerable:
          like candle flames caught in a wind
          in danger of extinction.
              How wrong to think you shrank
              from sharing wholly in our life.
          Loving God, in Christ you came to cast light into our darkness,
          laying yourself bare to the fickle whims of human passion.
          And in Christ you bore the pain of the Cross.
          You risked our rejection,
          for love of us, for our sake.
          Help us too to take the path of risky discipleship,
          for love of you, for your sake.

14   How easily this flame could be put out;
              one puff of wind,
              a finger tightly pressed against a thumb,
              then nothing.
          A man upon his cross; a flickering flame of life;
          how easily that life could be put out.
          Or so they said.
              Advent Promise; Christmas Lord; Easter Christ;
              you ever live in resurrection power.

15   *The people that walked in darkness have seen a great light; on those who lived in a land as dark as death, a light has dawned.*

Isaiah 9.2

One candle dispels the darkness:
Lord, be with us.
Add spark to our worship.
Make us lights for the world,
through Christ,
the Light that enlightens.

16   *I, the Lord have called you with a righteous purpose and taken you by the hand; I have formed you, and destined you to be a light for peoples, a lamp for nations.*

Isaiah 42.6

One candle dispels the darkness:
Lord, be with us.
Make our hearts burn within us,
so that we proclaim your word,
through Christ,
the Word made flesh.

17   *For in the tender compassion of our God, the dawn from heaven will break upon us, to shine on those who sit in darkness, under the shadow of death, and to guide our feet into the way of peace.*

Luke 1.78-79

One candle dispels the darkness:
Lord, be with us.
Shine like the dawn.
Colour our drab lives,
and help us to bring light into others' darkness,
through Christ,
the Light of the world.

18   *'I am the Lord's servant,' said Mary; 'may it be as you have said.'*

Luke 1.38

One candle dispels the darkness:
Lord, be with us.
Make our eyes shine with the light of hope.
Despite the cost to ourselves
or the fear of unknown pain,
help us to respond to your call
through Jesus,
Son of Mary.

19

Creative God,
out of blanket blackness
you conceived life;
bringing energy and light.
In the spinning earth
you were there in cycles and seasons,
giving purpose and plan.
We praise you for your creative power.

Redeeming God,
you did not remain aloof from your creation.
You committed yourself to individuals,
calling them to step out in faith.
You chose a nation to be your people
and brought them out of the land of slavery
with signs and wonders.
And then, beyond all expectation
you came in the person of Jesus of Nazareth.
We praise you for your redeeming love.

Sustaining God,
you continue your creative work,
you continue to redeem,
you have caught us up in your timeless purpose,
and drawn us into your covenant.
Creative, redeeming, sustaining God,
we worship you.

20

This Advent,
in our preparation
and in our waiting,
may we sense your continued work in our lives
and in the world around us.
For from ages past,
no ear has heard,
no mind has perceived,
no eye has seen
any God besides you,
who works for those who wait for him.
We anticipate your unfolding work
and we praise you.

21 Holy God,
for all your creation, we praise you:
    for the mind-bending curves of space and time,
      and for the sturdy simplicity of a blade of grass;
    for your care and correction through Covenant and Law,
      and through priest and prophet.
We praise you for your love now
    which prepares the way for us today,
      and helps us to see you more clearly.

Merciful God,
we praise you for your love for us shown in Jesus
    and we rejoice in his coming to share our life;
we give thanks for his redeeming death,
    and cling to the hope offered by his resurrection.
We praise you for the example of Jesus
    and that his living, dying and rising
    prepare the way for us to come into your presence,
    and learn to love you more dearly.

Mighty God,
we praise you for your coming to us in the Holy Spirit:
    uniting us in fellowship,
    inspiring our worship,
    guiding our lives
    and preparing the way for us,
    so that we may follow you more nearly,
    day by day.

22 God of grace, embracing us with hope,
    we worship and adore you.
God of mercy, rehearsing in us forgiveness,
    we worship and adore you.
God of peace, releasing us from sorrow,
    we worship and adore you.
Loving God, coming amongst us in Jesus Christ,
how can we but be moved to adore you?
    Your concern for us is complete.
    Your love of us without measure.
    Your trust in us more than we merit.
With all those who have marked Christ's coming, in all places and times,
we too would tell out our wonder, love and praise.
Through our one Lord, Jesus Christ.

23   Lord of holiness,
your hand spans the heavens
    and your arm is outstretched and strong.
You are beyond our imaginings
    and outside our senses.
Yet your reality breaks in:
    your majesty and power are reflected in the waterfall;
    your steadfastness in the mountain peak;
    and your shining beauty in the dewdrop and the morning frost.

Lord of love,
you came in Jesus to show how far you would travel with us:
    you are there in each act of our commitment,
    in every extra mile we travel
    and in every selfless act.
You walk with us in the breadth and variety of life,
    in every twinkling of an eye
    and in solemn seriousness.

Lord of hope,
you come ever closer to us,
    to guide and curb,
    inspire and challenge,
    to comfort and disturb.
You work with us to weave a pattern of life that pictures your glory.
And we adore.

24   God of light, source of love
and dispeller of darkness,
we welcome your coming and yet ...
    ... and yet your coming brings judgement.
    We prefer the darkness that covers our sin;
    the dawning light exposes our nakedness,
    the light of your love pierces us:
       disclosing pretension,
       revealing presumption.
    Like a laser it cuts to the heart of how we are and yet ...
    ... and yet that same light is not to burn us, but to heal us.
God of light, as day follows night,
and your coming heralds a new dawn of judgement, healing and hope,
so our hearts sing out in worship and adoration. In Jesus' name.

25

Forgive our timidity, loving God.
Forgive our desire to sail a smooth course
away from the storms of the world,
safe in a haven of holy contemplation.
Becalmed, we go nowhere,
except to drift on tides of passing fashion.
We too are of little faith,
and fear to lose our life
in the winds and rains of the world's reality.
Yet coming amongst us in Christ,
you spared yourself no pain
and sought no shelter.
Forgive us for failing to reflect Christ to the world.
Forgive us for fearing to risk rejection for Christ's sake.
Forgive us for safety-first discipleship,
for Christ's sake.

26

Loving God, we confess that we are not ready. We long to welcome once more the birth of your Son, but know that our faith is less than steadfast, our love less than strong, and our commitment less than sure.

Yet you love us as we are, and not alone for what we might become. You call us to repentance, and promise us forgiveness and guidance on the way of life. So, even in our lack of readiness, we give thanks that the child will come to his prepared cradle and bring the gift of renewal and the promise of grace.

27

Lord, we confess our impatience. We want you to act now, to transform the world and solve our problems. Yet we do not use the guidance and the resources you have already provided.

The world tells us that you are absent and that our faith is of no purpose, but we have done little to show them wrong. Our jaundiced politics and prejudiced theology have prevented us from recognizing the places where, and the people in whom, you are already at work.

Lord, forgive us. Help us to be patient and perceptive, and always alert to your action and purpose through Jesus Christ our Lord.

28

Lord, we hear
  you calling us to listen,
  urging us towards justice
  and bidding us to be a light for the nations.
But we fail,
and we know why we fail:
  we do not carry your teaching in our hearts;
  we are preoccupied with other business;
  we fear reproach;
  and worry what others will say.
Hunching our shoulders against the cold, and turning up our collars,
  we have turned in on ourselves,
  ignored the pressing needs of others,
  rejected the call to fairness,
  and thought the darkness not to be our concern.

Sometimes it feels as though we are groping in the dark,
  struggling on, hoping against hope,
  unwilling to face up to our failures and disappointments
  in case they drag us down and turn our world grey.
But then, caught by a quiet moment
or challenged by the glaring needs of human life,
we glimpse your love in Christ.
We see afresh the full possibilities of being human,
and realize anew what flickering shadows we are,
of all we could become.
And we are sorry:
  sorry for harsh words and neglected opportunities;
  sorry for acts of kindness left undone;
  sorry for the broken promises of discipleship.

Lord, lighten our darkness.
Let the bright shafts of your love gild our lives.
Let colour flood our greyness and sunbeams chase the sadness of our world.
Then we shall stand in the brightness of your presence
and reflect your glory, through Jesus Christ our Lord.

29
Forgiving God, we prepare to celebrate your coming amongst us,
yet in many ways we act as though you were an unwelcome guest.
You took the trouble to come close, like a child nestled in a woman's arms,
yet the cautious words we use to tell of you keep you at arm's length.
We are sorry.
Forgive us, Lord.

We say you are all knowing, intimately present in our lives,
yet we hide our inner feelings from you as though you were far distant.
We are sorry.
Forgive us, Lord.

We call you Lord and king,
yet keep areas of our lives closed to your influence,
and build barriers of self-interest as though we were defending private territory.
We are sorry.
Forgive us, Lord.

We celebrate the good news of your coming,
yet fail to share it with others.
We are sorry.
Forgive us, Lord.

> Lord, as Advent moves on and Christmas dawns,
> may we know your closeness,
> open our lives to you
> and share your love with others,
> in the name of Jesus Christ.

30
Lord, so often the fabric of our lives is imperfect:
tension pulls us out of shape;
cross words and unfinished conversations leave frayed edges;
broken relationships reveal hanging threads;
anger and scorn leave stains that we cannot shift on our own.
> Lord, forgive us, we are sorry.
> Gently clean us.
> Blow through us.
> Help us to stand again in your brilliance
> and reflect your glory.

31 For your coming in Christ among us
and for your measureless love of us,
  we thank you, God.
For your total commitment to us
and for your utter faithfulness to us,
  we thank you, God.
For your promise of peace within us
and for your healing of conflict between us,
  we thank you, God.
For your challenge of change set before us
and for your offered guidance to us,
  we thank you, God.

32 Lord, we give you thanks for your Spirit
    like living water within us,
    cleansing and refreshing,
    carrying us forward with power.
We give you thanks for Mary,
    who let your Spirit enter her life
    so that your presence grew in her
    and broke out into the world in Jesus Christ.

33 Loving God, we thank you for your love for us freely given. We don't deserve the grace you give us, but rejoice to receive it. We know we are unworthy of your favour but still you show it. We thank you that in Christ, you come into the chaos of our unreadiness, into the staleness of our self-regarding, into the endless distractions of our festivities, and love us. We rarely seem ready to receive you, yet you are resolutely ready to come. Loving God, we thank you, in Jesus' name.

34 For that conviction ever growing sure, that you will come;
For that strong hope that darkness will not last;
For that deep-flowing joy that earth will be refreshed;
For that awareness of the dawning light that tells of coming day;
  We thank you, Lord.

35

Lord Jesus Christ,
we thank you
that you took risks.
We thank you
that you shied from the easy road of compromise
and steadfastly walked the hard road of the Cross.
We thank you
that you shone the light of your love from Bethlehem to Calvary,
that in the face of indifference, rejection and death
still the flame of your love was not quenched.
We thank you,
and prepare ourselves to remember again your birth:
all that it still promises,
all that it still gives
and all that it still fires within us.
We thank you, our living Lord.

36

Eternal God, Lord of our lives,
we thank you for your coming in Christ.
In him new hope was seen
    by those the world despised.
In him new life was found
    by those the world dismissed.
In him new joy was known
    by those the world disowned.

And still you come in Christ,
still hope, life and joy
intrude gloriously into our world.
Still you turn us upside-down;
    lifting the humble
    and humbling the proud.
Still you raise the hearts of the downcast,
still you kiss the wounds of the outcast.
Eternal God, Lord of our lives,
we thank you.

37 Saving God, we prepare for your coming,
and long to see the signs of your Kingdom.

O come, O come Immanuel!
Ransom those in exile.
Care for those who have fled their homeland in fear.
Nurture those who live under oppressive regimes.
Give the marginalized the strength and assurance of your presence.
May all people find their true home in you!

O come, O come, Wisdom from above!
Guide all who govern the nations.
Be a sign of integrity for government ministers and civic leaders.
Deliver those in public service from corruption and time-serving.
Lead our politicians to honest goals without distorting truth.
May all people keep conscience pure and intention honourable!

O come, O come, Rod of Jesse!
Give kings, queens and presidents a sovereignty born of true humility.
Grant stability and continuity to faithful servants of the nations.
Number the citizens of our nation among the people of faith.
May all Christian people be a signpost to your royal throne!

O come, O come, Key of David!
Open the hearts of the hard-hearted and callous.
Unlock the unforgiving spirit and those held in the bonds of prejudice.
Proclaim again that the gates of heaven are open wide.
May the day come when all people find the hope of life beyond death!

O come, O come, Dayspring!
Let your morning light shine on those in dark depression.
Dawn with growing light on those engulfed in doubt.
Offer the springs of morning dew to those whose lives are like a parched
     land.
May all people walk out of the night-time of their fear into the light of your
     new day!

O come, O come, Immanuel!
Be born again in the Bethlehem of our time.
Live again in the Galilee of our generation.
And be raised high amongst us, by the power of God.
Jesus! Immanuel! Sign of the Kingdom! Come!

38   Eternal God, who spoke to Abraham words of friendship and promise,
      calling him to step out in faith into an uncertain future:
           we pray for those searching for a meaning to life;
           we pray for those worried about the future;
           we pray for those anchored in the past and lacking vision.

      Eternal God, who spoke to Moses, calling him to make the nation's promised
      future and guiding him to work for justice:
           we pray for leaders in the world and those who struggle to achieve
                liberty for the falsely imprisoned
                and justice for the oppressed;
           we pray for those involved in negotiations for peace;
           we pray for those who work to free people from the tyranny of addiction
           or the bondage of debt.

      Eternal God,
      who spoke words of healing through Christ,
           we pray for all who are ill or convalescing;
      who offered words of challenge through Christ,
           we pray for those who have not yet found the life of faith;
      who proclaimed words of hope through Christ,
           we pray for those who have lost all hope in others and in themselves.

      Eternal God, who spoke to Paul,
      transforming him from persecutor to evangelist:
           we pray for those who try to share the good news of your love with others
           we pray for the whole Church, seeking to interpret the relevance of the
                gospel message today.

      Eternal God, who spoke to John through vision and imagination:
           we pray for those who seek a vision of your future in our today;
           we pray for those who seek to be a part of your eternal plan;
           we pray for those who put flesh on your word and turn hope into action.

      Eternal God, who spoke in ancient times:
      speak your word in our time
      and give us ears to hear.
      In the name of Jesus Christ.

39 Loving God, darkness conceals so much pain.
In the soul's shadowland,
    the light of hope and love is spent,
    the agony of isolation cuts deeply,
    the pain of guilt cripples,
    the crude knife of injustice twists.

We pray for the lonely
    who know no friendship and share no joy;
    who feel forsaken and disregarded.
We pray for those who need to know forgiveness,
    yet fear to face their sin.
We pray for those oppressed and exploited,
    whose worth is thought so low.
In these Advent weeks,
we pray that the healing, judging and hope-bearing light
of our coming Christ
will dispel the darkness of their distress
and bring a dawn of renewal.

40 Mighty and merciful God,
you turn our expectations upside-down.
Show us how you can use us.
May your grace grow in us,
so that we may serve you,
through the power of the Holy Spirit.

41 Loving God,
we have met here as your people,
drawn together by your call
and built up by our response of faith.
You have united us
in the fellowship of the Holy Spirit.
As we go our separate ways,
may we be supported by each other
to be your people for the world,
through the power of your Spirit.

42 Expressive God,
we have heard your word,
may we learn to speak its truth.
We have been challenged by your call to action,
may we go out to do your will.
We have been inspired by your presence with us,
may we share your love with others,
through the power of your Spirit.

43 Challenging God,
in the face of failure and injustice,
help us to feel forgiven,
help us to make a fresh beginning
and confront the problems in our lives and in our world.
We look to meet you in our daily living
and know your Spirit with us and within us.

44 Go out to celebrate in love and laughter!
Go as lights for the world! Shine in the darkness!
Go out: act justly and walk humbly with our God!
Go in the name of him who loved and laughed,
who was the true light of the world
and humbled himself as a manger child.

45 God of grace,
as we are loved by you,
so teach us how to love;
as we are forgiven by you,
so help us to forgive;
as we are trusted by you,
so lead us to greater trust in you.
As we welcome the coming Christ,
so enliven us to reflect the living Christ
and become channels of hope to a broken world.

46 God of all our days,
    coming in Christ that our past be resolved,
    our present be proud
    and our future be assured,
    we commit ourselves to you.

    God of all our ways,
    coming in Christ that the poor be rich,
    the outcast embraced,
    the downcast uplifted,
    we commit ourselves to you.

    God of our lives,
    coming in Christ that we find life fulfilled,
    baptized into his death,
    raised to share his glory,
    we commit ourselves to you.

47 O God,
    houses and trees, buses and shops
    are silhouetted against a dark blue sky.
    As the lights of the town beckon,
    may your star of promise
    draw us onward and nearer our destination:
    to know more deeply who and where we are,
    to worship you and glorify your name for ever;
    through the Christ-child of Bethlehem.
    Crucified God, we ask this.

48
O lowly Christ;
on the darkest night of the year,
the Christmas moon
has laid a pathway
across the sea for you,
and the lighthouse
beams a welcome.

As sister moon gives way to brother sun,
the Prince of Peace is crowned.
Cries of pain give way to tears of joy
as Mary cradles the whole world in her arms.

A little child, a little child;
the living waters of Ezekiel
on Mary's knee.
O Saviour dear,
wise child of Isaiah;
help us to have the humility of the shepherds,
the wisdom of the wise,
the steadfast love of Joseph
and the courage of Mary.

O Alpha and Omega, on Mary's knee,
as your arm lifts the head of the guilty,
help us to forgive.
As your hands caress the faces of the poor,
help us to seek justice.
As you kiss the leper clean,
help us to know your peace.
O little child, root of Jesse,
promised one,
as we leave the stable,
as we go from Christmas into the New Year,
travel with us.

Christmas

49   The day before Christmas Eve;
an empty stable
bare, un-welcoming,
sits in an empty church.
> Soon the faithful, the curious and the hopeful will gather.
> Soon the church will be filled with warmth and praise:
> soft candlelight, children's voices, the song of the frosty stars.

And then the stable will be transformed,
filled with glory,
crowded with the Christmas cast
of donkeys and sheep,
shepherds and kings,
Mary, Joseph, and the Baby,
the Holy One of Israel,
asleep on the hay.
> Transform our empty spaces,
> O Christmas God.
> Fill the empty mangers of the world
> with food.
> Empty the cardboard boxes,
> refuge of the lonely and despairing.
> Bring warmth and light and shelter
> to all who watch and wait this night.
>> In bar and bare hillside,
>> in barrio and back room,
>> in crowded flat
>> and empty home,
>> may we feel your presence
>> at our shoulder and in our hearts.

And when the crib is packed away,
the figures carefully clothed
in protective covering,
unwrap the swaddling bands,
unfold the truth,
release the message: an empty stable –
> He's not here!
> He has risen!

50

Not beyond the earth,
not beyond the stars,
not cocooned in heaven,
not cradled in unconcern,
not you, God.

You are so committed to us
that you make our home, your home,
    our manger, your manger,
    our Bethlehem, your Bethlehem.

No more do we call you in from afar,
emergency technician for a broken-down world,
for now you are living with us:
listening, healing,
mending, forgiving,
teaching, sharing,
celebrating, suffering,
God with us, Immanuel.

May our worship this Christmas
reflect your closeness to us,
    your commitment to all people.

May your Word become flesh
in our bodies, minds and spirits,
so that our sad world may hear the glad song of the angels:
'Glory to God in the highest
and on earth peace!'

51

Tinsel and bright lights,
cash registers and credit cards,
food and drink.
    Our God calls us aside!
        to be still,
        to be at peace,
        to adore.
Our God, call us again,
to open our hearts and minds,
to hear again the message of Christmas.

52   Let us adore God, Creator, Son and Spirit.
'O come, let us adore him!'

God, we adore you,
voicing our amazement and wonder
at your patience through generation after generation.
Again and again
you could have given up on your people,
but you have renewed your covenant constantly.
At Christmas we are reminded of this miracle,
for the miracle has come to stay.

Let us adore God, the Creator of the universe.
'O come, let us adore him!'

Jesus, we adore you,
fragile child in a frightening world.
With shepherds we kneel in wonder;
with travellers we look on in amazement;
for you are a sign that we are adored by God,
            precious to him,
            worthy of a future.

Let us adore Jesus, Christ the Lord.
'O come, let us adore him!'

Holy Spirit, we adore you.
By your power, the life of God is moving among us.
You create newborn opportunities before our eyes;
you enter a mother's heart, a father's soul,
            and sow seeds of eternal hope;
you move in nations and kingdoms
            to transform history into a new era;
because of you, mothers, fathers, children
will never be the same,
for we shall all be changed.

Let us adore the Holy Spirit, life giver and transformer.
'O come, let us adore her!'

53 Lord God, you are the King of the universe;
    Glory!   **Glory, Alleluia!**

Lord God, you dwell in light and majesty;
    Glory!   **Glory, Alleluia!**

Lord God, you are beyond our highest thoughts;
    Glory!   **Glory, Alleluia!**

Lord God, you give light and life;
    Glory!   **Glory, Alleluia!**

Lord God, you did not forget us;
    Glory!   **Glory, Alleluia!**

You sent your Son to save us.
He is born, and lying in a manger;
    Glory!   **Glory, Alleluia!**

Lord God, we your people worship you;
    Glory!   **Glory, Alleluia!**

54 Welcome, Lord Jesus Christ!
No borders will contain you,
nothing will fence you in,
you will leap the boundaries that restrict.
    You are the Lord of space and distance.

Welcome, Lord Jesus Christ!
The changing seasons will not alter you,
day will not tire you, nor night oppress,
you will take the passing years in your stride.
    You are the Lord of time.

Welcome, Lord Jesus Christ!
No flags of nations will enfold you,
nothing of race or culture will distort you,
every needful human heart will hear your voice.
    You are the Lord of all.
Welcome, ever-welcome Lord!

55   Christmas Christ, what have we done to you?

You came in poverty,
   but we have turned Christmas into a shopping spree.
      Forgive us, we pray,
      Lord, forgive us.

You surprised the world by your coming,
   but we make it a routine, year after year.
      Forgive us, we pray,
      Lord, forgive us.

You summoned shepherds and foreigners to your celebration,
   but we often keep it to our families and friends.
      Forgive us, we pray,
      Lord, forgive us.

You take enormous risks to be with us,
   but we are obsessed with our own comfort and joy.
      Forgive us, we pray,
      Lord, forgive us.

You come with a message of costly peace,
upsetting the proud, encouraging the weak,
   but we hope that things will go on as usual.
      Forgive us, we pray,
      Lord, forgive us.

Inspire us this Christmas,
so that we appreciate afresh the meaning of your coming,
transforming our individual lives and communities
into signs of your active reign among us.

Let forgiveness be your Christmas gift to us,
and new commitment be our Christmas gift to you.

56   Father, your Son was born into a world no more fair than our own,
    yet retained his integrity,
    renewed hope and love,
    and re-created a vision of the world
        as you intended it to be.

Father, this is still an unfair world;
it is not the world you planned
and we confess that we have not been amongst the first to make it better.
It is Christmas,
    and we spend more on presents than some earn in a year;
    we decorate our houses whilst others have no shelter;
    we over-eat whilst others starve;
    we settle for complacent peace
    whilst many live with intolerance and oppression.

Lord, forgive us and help us use this Christmas
to re-think our place and calling
in your world.

57   Lord, how costly this Christmas is!
But for all the wrong reasons:
    cards and cake,
    tinsel and trees,
    driving and drink,
    parties and presents.

Forgive us, Lord.
Show us now the cost of a true Christmas:
    love and listening,
    care and comfort,
    help and healing,
    giving and gratitude,
    denial and death.

Forgive us, Lord, so that renewed,
we may find the Christmas that leads to Easter
and thus meet it with costly love.

58 Gracious God,
our hearts rejoice, our spirits leap for joy
because you have rescued us and set us free.

What was hidden has come into the open;
what was distorted has been put right;
what was impossible has happened before our eyes.

You have come as you said you would,
but not as we had predicted.

We thank you for entering our life completely,
     making holy
     our bodies, our communities, our families,
     our eating, our resting, our sleeping,
     our waiting, our longing, our preparing,
     our night, our day,
     our work, our play,
     our hopes, our fears,
     our joys, our tears.

We thank you for coming as a child,
     reminding us
     that each human life is precious,
     that we depend totally on your goodness,
     that we rely on each other to live and survive,
     that we grow in your love and wisdom.

We thank you for choosing Bethlehem,
     the place of coming and going,
     the place of foreign oppression,
     the place where Ruth and Naomi were welcomed,
     the place of travellers and seekers.

We thank you that Christmas each year
     is an opportunity:
     for retelling the story,
     for giving and receiving,
     for worship and song
     and for renewal and re-dedication.

59   HOPE   We pray for all who hope for good news,
         even when it does not come;
    for all who hope for healing,
         even though they are still anxious.
We pray for all who have lost hope for their children
    because they are surrounded by disease,
    by famine, by war, by vendetta.
We pray for all who build hope
    by identifying with the hopeless;
    by living alongside the desperate;
    by kissing the weeping child
    and hugging the grief-stricken mother.

     PEACE   We pray for peace this Christmas:
    peace on earth as it is in heaven,
    peace in our homes, peace in our cities,
    peace in war zones, peace in feuding families,
    peace outside us, peace inside us,
    peace between nations, peace between religions.
We pray for peace-creators and peace-destroyers,
    peace-protectors and peace-disturbers,
    peace-enablers and peace-breakers.

     LOVE   We pray this Christmas for lovers:
    lovers of hope and lovers of peace,
    lovers of friends and lovers of enemies,
    lovers of the loveless and lovers of those injured,
    lovers of life and lovers of justice,
    lovers of animals and lovers of creation,
    lovers of beauty, lovers of music, lovers of art,
    lovers of babies in straw-filled mangers,
    lovers of worship and lovers of generosity.

In the name of Jesus,
    hope-giver,
    peace-maker,
    love-bringer,
       we offer these prayers.

60

Fun and food, family and friends;
that's the picture of Christmas
and we are glad of it.
Yet, we pause, for not everyone is in the frame.
Here and now, in the midst of our excitement,
we remember how others must spend this day
to give us our picture of happiness.

We remember those for whom this day brings work, not relaxation:
    those who work in the essential services;
        electricity, gas and water,
    those who care for our safety;
        police and fire brigade officers,
        ambulance and medical workers,
        doctors and nurses,
    those who bring us pleasure;
        entertainers, radio and television technicians,
and all others who must work to make our time a day of rest.

We remember those for whom this day brings separation
rather than family meeting:
    students, visitors, immigrants and refugees from overseas;
    people from our own country who are abroad;
        families emigrated, holiday-makers and those who serve them,
        soldiers, sailors and airforce personnel,
    those detained for our or their own safety;
        prisoners in jails, young people in detention centres,
        children in local authority care
        and all their families,
and all others separated from those whom they care for, and love.

We remember all those for whom this day brings sorrow rather than joy:
    the sick and dying, at home or in hospice and hospital;
    those who have fallen through the net of social care;
        the homeless, families in bed and breakfast accommodation,
        those driven from home by obsessive addictions,
    those with painful memories;
        of loved ones who have died in this last year,
        of better times when life was sweet,
and for all who feel isolated and lonely.

May the birth of Jesus move us from prayer to action.

61 Father, your Son Jesus came to a world where many knew a paralysing fear, and the shadow of Herod's sword fell even across the manger bed. And still fear lives on in human hearts. In the quietness of our worship we remember people who live in fear this Christmas-time.

We pray for
>   those who fear oppression and warfare;
>   those who fear religious or political intolerance;
>   those who fear discrimination because of their colour, race, or gender;
>   those who fear that their hunger or sickness will never go away.

We pray for
>   little children fearful of abuse by trusted relatives;
>   women fearful of a partner's violence;
>   those in inner cities, or high-rise flats fearful to leave their homes;
>   the elderly or frail fearful even in the shelter of their own house.

As Jesus met the human fears around him,
presenting the power of God's love,
so may your Church offer the love of God
>   to meet the inner needs of individuals,
>   and create communities of care in which love casts out fear.

62 Father, it is difficult to step into someone else's shoes and share their life. Yet in Jesus you immersed yourself in our very being, fully sharing our life. Help us this Christmas-time to re-dedicate ourselves to the service of men, women and children and so follow in the steps of the child who is our Lord.

63 As Jesus brought peace, turn us into peacemakers.
As Jesus brought hope, make us messengers of hope.
As Jesus brought love, rekindle love in us
so that the birth of the baby in Bethlehem
may be a beginning
and not an end.

64   Living God,

may the worship we have shared this Christmas

lead to acts of service which transform people's lives;

may the carols we have sung this Christmas

help others to sing, even in their sadness;

may the gifts we have exchanged this Christmas

deepen our spirit of giving throughout the year;

may the candles we have lit this Christmas

remind us that you intend no one to live in darkness;

may the new people we have met this Christmas

remind us that we meet you in our neighbours;

may the gathering together of family and friends this Christmas

make us appreciate anew the gift of loved ones;

may the stories we have told again this Christmas

be good news of great joy to us and all people

on our lips and in our lives;

may the ways you have come close to us this Christmas

not be forgotten

but, hidden in our memories,

be a rich resource

to lift us when times are painful

and humble us when things go well,

for you are our life, our light and our salvation

this season and always,

because of Jesus Christ our Lord.

Epiphany

65   Bright morning star, shine in our hearts:
   bring light for our darkness.

   Sun of righteousness, warm our world:
   bring healing for our wounds.

   Child of tomorrow, pitch your tent here today:
   bring joy for our sorrow.

   Christ of the cosmos, transform heaven and earth:
   bring hope for our desolation.

66   Star child,
      wanted and welcomed by the humble,
      hated and hounded by power-seekers:
            refuge and refugee,
               we love you!

            Apple of God's eye,
      cherished and chosen by Kingdom-travellers,
      rejected and ridiculed by the earth-bound:
            sacred and scarred,
               we honour you!

            Light of the world,
      tended and treasured by the pure in heart,
      shadowed and shunned by the deceitful:
            peerless and pierced,
               we exalt you!

67   God of wisdom, we too would be wise,
   but we admit our failures of imagination,
   our tactless blundering in the court of Herod,
   our setting in train the slaughter of the innocents.

      Forgive us for our not-looking –
   our enthusiasm for goods where over-production means
   felled forests, a polluted environment, stolen land,
      sweated labour and separated families.

Forgive us for our not-looking –
our insistence on high standards when this means
knowledge withheld from the poor, care postponed for the voiceless,
    and the stockpiling of basic resources.

    Forgive us for our not-looking –
our zeal for conversion campaigns when this means
censure of other faiths, loss of cultural richness, persecution of prophets
    and an alienation of minorities.

Forgive us:
    we do not mean to do harm,
    we do not mean to lack compassion.
Too late we notice and understand the tears we have caused
    and are ashamed.

Create us anew:
give us eyes to see, ears to hear,
hearts to care, minds to comprehend.
May Christ transform our grave mistakes,
that the deserts we have caused may blossom as the rose.

68   God of near and far,
we thank you that the wise men crossed boundaries
of territory, culture, religion and tradition,
that these strangers became friends as they knelt beside the crib.

God of logic and intuition,
we thank you that the wise men lifted their eyes
above their books, their conscious knowledge and their ordered lives,
that these thinkers became dreamers as they knelt beside the crib.

God of affluence and want,
we thank you that the wise men brought precious gifts:
gold for majesty, frankincense for contemplation, myrrh for suffering,
that these rich ones knew their poverty as they knelt beside the crib.

God of stranger and friend, thinker and dreamer, rich and poor,
thank you for showing us your nature, your vision, your love,
    as we too kneel beside the crib.

69   Thank you, scandalous God,
> for giving yourself to the world,
> not in the powerful and extraordinary,
> but in weakness and in the familiar:
> in a baby; in bread and wine.

Thank you
> for offering at journey's end, a new beginning;
> for setting, in the poverty of a stable,
> the richest jewel of your love;
> for revealing, in a particular place,
> your light for all nations.

Thank you
> for bringing us to Bethlehem, House of Bread,
> where the empty are filled,
>   and the filled are emptied;
> where the poor find riches,
>   and the rich recognize their poverty;
> where all who kneel and hold out their hands,
>   are unstintingly fed.

70   Journeying God, who beckons us to join you on the road,
be with all your people as we set out into this new year.

Give courage to the cautious,
> strength to the weary,
> vision to the short-sighted,
> hope to those who are broken in spirit.

When we are unsure of where you are leading
and cannot chart our path or progress,
give us trust and a toleration of not knowing.

When we are certain about the pattern of your mission,
give us humility – and the grace
to listen and learn from each new situation.

As the wise men brought gifts to the Christchild,
so may we bring gifts to one another in the world:
> **Gold:** May we share material resources justly;
>> practise fair trade; respect the earth
>> and exercise mutual deference.
> **Frankincense:** May we promote freedom of thought, speech and worship;
>> find opportunities for all to grow in grace and stature;
>> take quietness with us wherever we go;
>> and exercise mutual encouragement.
> **Myrrh:** May we stand in solidarity with the oppressed and suffering;
>> weep with those who weep; lament the atrocities of history;
>> bring balm for tomorrow
>> and exercise mutual love.

Journeying God, help us to follow you, however risky it seems, for in you lies
our ultimate security, our greatest freedom.

71

Beckoning God,
who called the rich to travel towards poverty,
> the wise to embrace your folly,
> the powerful to know their frailty;
who gave to strangers
> a sense of homecoming in an alien land;
and to star-gazers
> true light and vision as they bowed to earth;
we lay ourselves open to your signs for us.

Stir us with holy discontent over a world
which gives its gifts to those
> who have plenty already,
> whose talents are obvious,
> whose power is recognized;
and help us
both to share our resources with those who have little
and to receive with humility the gifts they bring to us.

Rise with us like a star
and make us restless
till we journey forth
to seek our rest in you.

72   Epiphany is a jewel,
multi-faceted,
flashing colour and light.
Epiphany embraces
the nations of the world,
kneeling on a bare floor
before a child.
Epiphany shows
a man
kneeling in the waters of baptism.
Epiphany reveals
the best is kept for last,
as water becomes wine
at the wedding feast.
> O Holy One
> to whom was given
> the gifts of power and prayer,
> the gift of suffering;
> help us to use
> these same gifts
> in your way
> and in your name.

73   God of light,
shed on the world through Christ,
we pray that we bear Christ's light to the world.
As the rising sun burns away the night's darkness
to bring a dawn of fresh life,
so we pray that we speak and live the gospel's promise
of rising hope;
of judgement and of joy and of life reborn.
For the sake of Christ our light.

74 God-with-us, Immanuel,
we have no gold,
no frankincense,
no myrrh.
But we bring you
our homage,
our prayers,
our self-denial,
poor and pale though they are,
knowing you will not turn us away
but will hold out your arms
to welcome us home.

75 What can we bring to your sufficiency but our poverty?
What can we bring to your beauty but our wretchedness?
What can we bring to your wholeness but our woundedness?

Made poor, wretched and wounded for our sakes,
you welcome us wherever we are, whatever we bring.

76 Our singing heart, our day's doxology, our gold,
we bring for celebration.
Our stillness, our glimpses of serenity, our frankincense,
we bring for meditation.
Our brokenness, our tears of rage and sorrow, our myrrh,
we bring for sacrifice.

Lent

77   God, whose touchstone is the desert and the cross,
draw near with your ancient strength
which we experience but do not understand,
know, but never see.
  Accompany us throughout the weeks of Lent,
  that we may face the demons, fantasies and fears
  which accompany us; so that, journeying with Jesus
  in desert places, we may by your mercy renew
  our commitment to the life of Christ
  and our vocation to the way of the Cross.

78   Into a dark world
a snowdrop comes,
a benison
of hope and peace,
carrying within it
a green heart,
symbol of God's renewing love.

Come to inhabit our darkness,
Lord Christ,
for dark and light
are alike to you.

May nature's white candles of hope
remind us of your birth,
and lighten our journey
through Lent and beyond.

79   God,
             journey with us
             as we remember why your Son
             turned his back on Galilee
             and strode towards Jerusalem.
             Journey with us,
             and open our eyes
             to see his mind, his heart, his dedication,
                   his worries, his fears, his questions,
                   his love, his single-mindedness, his sacrifice.

             Come, by your Spirit,
             and within our worship and prayers,
             speak to our deepest selves,
             so that Jesus' friendship and example
             may be so impressed on our experience
             that our own dreaming and deciding
             will draw strength, wisdom and insight.

             May this Lent be a time of sacrifice:
                   the making sacred of each moment, hour and day;
                   the making holy of our relationships,
             in the way of Jesus Christ our Lord.

80   Calling God, you whose breath
             is as hot and searching as desert wind,
             yet cool and refreshing as morning dew;
             we are amazed that in your strength
             you do not overwhelm us,
             nor in your tenderness
             hold back the piercing word.
                   You invite us to meet you in barren, lonely places
                   and to discover them to be gardens of growth.
             Our 'Yes' to you today is our adoration,
             for faced with such glory, we can but say
             Yes, Yes, Yes!

81

Jesus,
striding Saviour,
you puzzle us and you amaze us!
The word 'safety' is not in your vocabulary;
self-preservation is not on your agenda.

> You fill us with delight,
>   but also with trepidation.
> You brighten our days with your wisdom,
>   but we remain ignorant of your intentions.
> You heal and help, you welcome and embrace,
>   but we fear where all this will lead.

God of Jesus, we call to you in worship.
Shed light upon us this Lent
so that we may not only walk with Jesus your Son,
but begin to understand why he journeyed,
                    why he suffered
                and why he died.

Then prepare us in heart and mind
to be friends of Jesus in the places where we live,
so that if we have to face our Jerusalems,
we will have his courage,
            his sense of justice
        and his gift of forgiveness.
We ask this in his name.

82

As surely as the seasons unfold
and spring follows winter,
so sure is your steadfast love,
O God.
As rivers
released from winter's bondage
leap joyously to the sea,
melt our frozen hearts
that we may worship you.

83   Patient God,
you know us through and through;
you know our motives and our dreams;
you know our apathy and indifference;
you see beneath our shallow self-confidence;
underneath, our lives are weak and flimsy.
We hide our true selves behind busyness and bravado;
we worship our own egos, our bank balances, our careers.

Like Simon Peter, our rocky exteriors crumble
under the pressure of opposition.

Like James and John, we long for the rewards of the Kingdom
without the struggle of the journey.

Like all the disciples, we want success not failure;
we want all the hard work to end in recognition and acclaim.

Forgive us for our blindness. It goes on and on.

Where are we to go?
You have the words of eternal life.

84   Deep in our lives the hidden rumblings of our
regret and remorse reside.
God of desert heat and silent honesty, shine upon us for we have:
    spoken of peace but failed to live it;
    confessed Christ but refused the cross
    which came in the form of our neighbours
    or out of our neighbourhoods.
We often fail to recognize Christ
in the wilderness today,
and resist ministering to him
in harrowing poverty close at hand.
    Forgive us and renew us,
    for even in our failure
    we do remain true to you.
Desert Christ, visit us with the living stream
of your forgiveness.

85

As buds uncurl
and flowers open their faces to the sun,
turn us
to the light and warmth
of your presence,
that in confidence
we may confess our sin:

Silence

God of justice, peace and love,
we knock at your gate
with our prayers:
we confess that our lives
and the life of the world
are broken apart
by our sin.

But Jesus said: 'Behold I stand at the door and knock.'
As we open the door to justice,
    we ask to be forgiven.
As we open the door to peace,
    we ask to be renewed.
As we open the door to love,
    we ask to be made whole.

86

Thank you, Jesus:
        for not turning stones into bread,
        for not jumping off the temple roof,
        for not being a wonder boy.

Thank you, Jesus:
        for not accepting the golden crown,
        for not taking authority over earthly kingdoms,
        for not joining the nationalist movement.

Thank you, Jesus:
> for choosing the way of service
>> rather than domination;
> for choosing the long, slow road
>> rather than that of instant solutions;
> for choosing loyalty to your Father's Kingdom
>> rather than personal acclaim and approval.

Thank you, Jesus:
> for being a true Israelite,
> a child of the wilderness
> where all defences disappear
> and all living things are fragile.

Thank you, Jesus:
> for facing hot and cold;
>> good and evil;
>> life and death;
>> yes and no;
> forty days and forty nights.

Thank you, Jesus:
> for showing Satan the door
> so that we can face our wilderness decisions
> with greater vision and courage.

87 Father, we are glad that you offer times to stop and think.
As Lent returns we pause in our journey,
and thank you:
> for your costly commitment to us in Jesus Christ;
> for the gospel stories that declare your love;
> for opportunities of talking together about our faith
> and for times of personal prayer and reflection.

We thank you where your Church
> has been prepared to take risks,
> suffer for the work of your Kingdom,
> and that we are a part of its journeying life.

As we discover more about your love,
help us to show our thankfulness
by putting that same love into action
in our lives.

88   God,
in Jesus you have entered the world's wilderness
   and ventured into the dark and thorny places,
      the forbidden and forbidding places,
      the hot and hungry places,
         and therefore you have heard
         the cries of the starving;
      you have experienced
         the agonies of the uprooted and nationless;
      you have encountered
         the plight of the tormented in body and mind.

Hear us once more
as we hold out to you, in our arms and in our prayers,
all those children of the wilderness
who are desperate in their struggles.

Give to us a conscience like that of Jesus
   and a compassion like yours
so that the wilderness of this world
may begin to blossom and flower
and all may have the gifts you give to life –
   water, health, shelter and peace.

Disturb our comforts until we care,
disturb our governments until they respond,
so that for those who are fragile and powerless,
     exiled and downtrodden,
     grief-stricken and depressed,
   the forty days and forty nights will be over.

89   *The following prayer is intended to be used after reading the story of the temptations*
of Jesus.   *(Matthew 4.1-11; Luke 4.1-13)*

Dragons lurk in desert spaces
penetrating the mind with evil claw.
Tempting, probing,
wrestling, pleading;
   doubts undermine the sense of call
   and twist the focus of obedience.

Such is the pain of the wilderness.
Alone, alone, alone,
Christ sits
in the waste place of abandoned pleas and questions
until exhausted.
Finally,
at last,
the realization
comes
that in the end
there is only
God.

In the night-time of our fears,
and in our time of questioning,
be present, ever-present God.
Be present with those
camped out in the fields of hopelessness
and with those who live lives of quiet desperation.
Be present until the desert places
blossom like the rose
and hope is born again.

90   We pray for those who cannot walk the Lenten road.
          How can they fast to show the discipline of faith
              when fasting is their daily life,
              starvation ever close,
              and thirst is barely quenched;
                  the well is dry?
          How can they make a busy diary clear,
          to offer time for service, prayer and thought,
              when every desert day is tedium-long,
              stretched out by unemployment and the loss of work,
              and one day stands as did the last,
              and will the next?
      Lord, whilst we thank you for the luxury of Lent;
      and every call to discipline it brings,
      we pray for those who know its call too well,
      and live it every day.

91 Lord Jesus, walking the painful road that led to your cross, still you took time to respond to the people you met. Our road is broader, its end more clear, our burdens lighter. Help us to meet the needs of those we meet.

We pray for those for whom the roadside is their only home, for those in towns and cities who sleep in shop doorways, for those who beg for our small change or sell the *Big Issue.*

We pray for people for whom the road is a place of injury or death, and those bereaved by road accidents.

We pray for people for whom the road presents an opportunity, those moving to new jobs, travelling to meet friends or to discover the world.

We pray for those for whom the road ahead seems closed, those in despair or suffering from depression, those who have no opportunity to use their skills in employment, those trapped in false relationships, or whose situation is a seeming cul-de-sac.

Help us to see people rather than problems.

As sisters and brothers of the travelling Christ, help us to support and encourage each other along the way. Give us love enough to stop and care for those with whom we journey.

92 Lord God, your commitment to us is clear:
    we see it in the ministry of Jesus.
Your commitment to us is complete:
    we see it in the crucifixion of Jesus.

Our commitment to you is often mixed:
    what do we want for ourselves;
        what shall we give to you?
    Shall we serve you with unmeasured love;
        shall we give you a part, and keep a part?

Help us in this time of Lent to walk with Jesus on his Calvary journey so that our commitment is clear and our love complete.

93   Lord, we would stay in Galilee
where the fishing is good
and the people are crowding to see you,
but you have other priorities:
it's time to move on and respond to the call.
   Help us to rise up and follow.

Lord, we would stay at Caesarea Philippi
where it's safe and we can talk in peace,
but you have other priorities:
Jerusalem waits for a saviour.
   Help us to rise up and follow.

Lord, we would stay on the Mount of Transfiguration
where we can worship the past
and glory in the present,
but you have other priorities:
down below an epileptic boy needs healing.
   Help us to rise up and follow.

Lord, we would stay at Bethany
where the hospitality is good
and there are friends and laughter,
but you have other priorities:
the world needs to see how God loves.
   Help us to rise up and follow.

94   As the heralds of spring
golden-trumpet
the arrival of Easter,
as the dark night of Lent passes
and the days lengthen,
so we would become
your Easter people, O Christ.
Shepherds of your sheep,
peacemakers and hospitality-givers,
open to change and partnership,
Spirit-led, in solitude and costly service.

The Life of Jesus

95

Faithful God,
we come looking to Jesus; the pioneer and perfecter of our faith.
We come to draw the threads of lives together, and find wholeness.
May your Spirit be with us as it was in Jesus:
    holding all together in harmony:
        the human with the divine,
        the stillness of being with the energy of doing,
        speaking with acting,
        death with resurrection.

Faithful God,
you show your faith in us
by making us partners in your work,
and calling us to continue Christ's mission.
Be with us now,
give us integrity, bring us to wholeness,
so that our faith may show in quiet and action,
as following the way of Christ,
we reach maturity in him.

96

Jesus our brother,
God who came as one of us,
you stand with us in the struggles of life:
in peace and relaxation,
and in the salt of sweat and the pain of tears.
Encourage and strengthen us.
Bless and question us.
Through you we know God:
    you are the smiling eyes of God,
    you are the burning heart of God's love.
Your obedience is our example
and we praise your name.

97

O Christ, friend of sinners,
as you called men and women
into community with you,
call us to be your fisher people.
Gather us from our present occupation
to focus on the needs of your world.

Forgive us the pride and avarice
that keep us from you.
Forgive us the greed
that pollutes rivers and seas.
Forgive us the fear
that leads to war.

98   Lord Jesus Christ,
you saw the vast sweep of God's purpose
    but we have been preoccupied with details,
    anchored in the trivial,
    and have failed to grasp a vision
    of your work in the world.

Yours was a total commitment to each person you met
    but we have been insensitive even to those close to us.
We have not pulled our weight,
    and we have looked to our own interests.
We have seen our religion as an end in itself,
    rather than a springboard to a new life.

You showed that love was the real power of human life
    but we have used power to dominate others
    and even our weakness has become a tool to manipulate friendship.
Our love has not always led to responsibility,
    and we have failed to encourage good.

We are sorry.
Forgive us, and lead us to better ways.

99   Gracious God,
for your love for us,
gentle as a shower,
healing our pain,
binding our wounds,
    we give you thanks.

For your love for us,
sure as the dawn,
transforming our darkness,
revealing your truth,
    we give you thanks.

For your love for us,
mercifully steadfast,
calling us to you,
raising us up,
    we give you thanks.

For your love for us,
encouraging questions,
open to doubts,
making us vulnerable,
    we give you thanks.

    Urge us on, O Christ,
    to find wholeness
    through serving you
    by serving others,
    in the power of your Spirit.

100 To you, Lord Jesus Christ, thanksgiving and praise!
Your life touches ours at so many points.
Thank you for lighting up our thoughts,
our feelings and our wills.
Focus your light in our lives, like a healing laser,
so that your love shines out through us to others:
    cast out fear with your love,
    transfigure despair with your hope,
    and to confusion, bring your clarity,
    so that our thanksgiving is endless.

101   Lord, we bring the world's complex sadness to you. As we see your compassion in the life of Christ, so we trust to see your involvement in the lives of ordinary people in their trouble. Where else would we go? You have the words of eternal life.

Jesus said, 'I am the bread of life'.
We pray for those who are hungry:
>   hungry because crops have failed,
>   hungry because of war,
>   hungry because of unfair trading arrangements.
We pray for those who hunger and thirst for righteousness.
May they be satisfied.

Jesus said, 'I am the light of the world'.
We pray for those who live in darkness:
>   the darkness of oppression,
>   the darkness of threat or violence,
>   the darkness of injustice.
We pray for those overwhelmed by the darkness of depression.
May they find relief.

Jesus said, 'I am the good shepherd'.
We pray for those who have lost their way:
>   lost in loneliness and isolation,
>   lost in a crowd,
>   lost along life's journey.
We pray for those who have never truly found their place in life.
May the good shepherd find and lead them.

Jesus said, 'I am the resurrection and the life'.
We pray for those who fear that death has the final say:
>   fearful because a loved one has died,
>   fearful of their own life's ending,
>   fearful that grief will overtake them.
May they clearly hear the promise of abundant life.

Jesus said, 'I am the true vine'.
We pray for those with no firm hold on life:
>   insecure because they are homeless,
>   insecure because they have been driven from their homeland,
>   insecure because their lives seem barren rather than fruitful.
May they find security in Christ and a sense of belonging in the Church.
We offer these prayers in the name of Jesus, the way, the truth, and the life.

102 God our Father, you gave yourself to the world in Jesus
to make a way for us to reach you.
Now as the body of Christ,
may we give ourselves in service,
proclaiming the good news of your love,
and being your people in the world.

103 Flash of insight,
Surging hope,
Jab of conscience,
Quiet reflection;
 God within us,
 Come, call us to new obedience,
And give us strength to follow.

Word of prophet,
Depth of wisdom,
Strength of long years,
Reformation;
 God in history,
 Come, call us to new obedience,
And give us strength to follow.

Psalm's rejoicing,
 Sanctuary stillness,
 Chorus praising,
 Bible searching;
  God in church and temple,
  Come, call us to new obedience,
And give us strength to follow.

Flesh of our flesh,
Word appearing,
Love in action,
Death and new birth;
 God in Jesus,
 Come, call us to new obedience,
And give us strength to follow.

Jesus:

Healer, Teacher and

Friend

104 Gracious God,
Lord of light,
shining on the world,
we join our voices to praise you.

In Jesus Christ
your glory has risen on us,
our light has come.
So we can learn and grow:
    we can sing, we can celebrate;
    we can pray, we can listen again;
    and be healed from sorrow and anxiety;
    our joy made full.

Christ, our light,
shines on our lives.
Our faith is brighter
and our understanding clearer.
We gather to praise,
in Jesus' name.

105 Come and teach us, Lord Jesus:
without you we do not know how to worship God
with all our heart and mind.

Come and teach us, Lord Jesus:
without you we do not know how to pray with commitment and passion.

Come and teach us, Lord Jesus:
without you we cannot understand God's word to us.

Come and teach us, Lord Jesus:
without you we cannot love ourselves and each other.

Come and teach us, Lord Jesus:
without you we do not know how to work for the Kingdom.

Come and teach us, Lord Jesus,
so that this church and everyone who is a part of it
may become more like you.

106 Loving God, we gather in Jesus' name:
bringing our hungry hearts and carrying our heavy loads.
We come to find rest and life.
We come to drink of the living water that is Jesus your Son.
He will sustain us, and help us grow in faith and understanding.
Bless us as we do.
In Jesus' name.

107 Come, our friend calls to us.
Come, our friend has time for us.
Come, our friend speaks to us.
Come to Jesus, our friend.
    Jesus, we answer your call.
    Jesus, we have time for you.
    Jesus, we hear your word.
    We come to you, Jesus our friend.

108 Jesus, you were a friend to the disciples,
you taught them, you guided them, you loved them.
As we meet in worship,
teach us, guide us, love us.

Jesus, you were a friend to the outcast and sinner,
you called them, you challenged them, you forgave them.
As we pray to you,
call us, challenge us, forgive us.

Jesus, you were a friend to the sick,
you touched them, healed them, restored them.
As we seek you today,
touch us, heal us, restore us.

Jesus, you are our friend,
bind us to each other and to you,
so that your love for us
may be reflected in our love for all.

109 Loving God,
great in love, wisdom and might,
majestic without compare;
we worship you.
You are the Creator – flinging stars into space,
bringing the light of life
to the darkness of barren waste.

God of compassion,
comforter of wounded souls,
meeting pain with peace, and woe with joy,
turning pride and power upside-down
and lifting humble hearts high;
we worship you.
You are the Redeemer – rescuing us from sin and shame,
bringing the promise of forgiveness
to the despair of guilt.

God of liberation,
lifting lives crushed by circumstance,
filling hearts fearful of worth,
raising hopes dashed by sorrow;
we worship you.
You are the Inspirer – urging pilgrims on,
to find the Way, Truth and Life
for all their days.

We worship and adore you.
In Christ's name.

110 Jesus, we stand amazed at the quality of your friendship:
you are loyal and constant in your relationship with us,
you are compassionate and caring in our time of need,
you offer prayer and action so that thought and deed become one.

Jesus, we worship and adore you for your unreserved offering of yourself to each
one of us as individuals, and to your Church – your community of friendship.

111 Merciful God,
we rejoice that your purpose for us is life:
casting light into our darkness,
bringing order from our chaos,
breathing life into barren souls.
God of life, we adore you.

Compassionate God,
we rejoice that your offer to us is new life:
calling us to confession,
holding out forgiveness,
freeing us from guilt.
God of new life, we adore you.

Inspiring God,
we rejoice that your promise to us is full life:
giving purpose to our days,
bearing fruits from Spirit-gifts,
guiding us to live love's truth.
God of full life, we adore you.
In Christ's name.

112 God of our bodies,
you made us to praise and adore you.
We praise you that your great longing for us
came to fulfilment through the body of Mary
and that of her son, Jesus.

In his flesh you honoured our living;
through his flesh you shared our joy and sorrow.
From his flesh came your healing life,
and still it comes.

Upon this day we cannot but adore you,
for in Jesus the spark from eternity touches our flesh
and renews creation.

113 Your love is for children whatever their age;
Jesus the friend of all: **We worship you.**

You show concern for the sick in body, mind or spirit;
Jesus the friend of all: **We worship you.**

You share the loneliness of the rejected and isolated;
Jesus the friend of all: **We worship you.**

You break down barriers of race, religion and age;
Jesus the friend of all: **We worship you.**

You rejoice when we seek to follow your way, your truth and your life;
Jesus the friend of all: **We worship you.**

114 We praise you, Loving God, for friends.
For the people who love us
with a love that is overflowing, unending,
given without seeking anything in return.

We praise you, Loving God, for Jesus.
For the way he loves us
with a love which is more wonderful than any human love,
given freely so that we might know you as our friend.

We praise you, Loving God, for our love.
For the way we have been shown how to love
by our parents, our neighbours,
by our Christian brothers and sisters.
For the way we have been taught how to love
by Jesus, the friend of all.
For the impulse to love
planted in us by your Spirit.

We praise you, Loving God,
for friendship makes us the people we are.

115 Lord Jesus, the friendship you offered was unreserved. You set no limits, created no boundaries; whatever the need of the man, woman or child, you responded, offering the kind of friendship which was right for them.

You expected your followers to do the same!
Your first disciples found it hard.
We find it almost impossible.

Jesus, friend of all, forgive us that so often we limit our friendship to those who offer us friendship; forgive us that we treat people as statistics and problems, not as human beings with needs just like our own.

As we ask for forgiveness, we also pray for the power of your Holy Spirit in our lives, that we may be enabled to see individual people through your eyes, and then reach out with your sensitive friendship.

116 You said it, Lord!
　　'Love you enemies as your friends.'
　　'Love your neighbour as yourself.'
　　'Love the Lord your God with all your heart.'

Hard words; hard words to follow.
　　You command us to love,
　　but so often we are only half-hearted in our love.
It is easier to make enemies than make friends;
easier only to look after ourselves than care for neighbours;
easier to ignore you than serve you.

We are sorry,
for the many times when we fail to follow your commands,
for the many ways we have failed to love as we are loved,
for our many failures to accept and acknowledge your great love.

Loving God, your Son was a friend to sinners,
and in love gave even his life for his friends.
In his name we ask for forgiveness.
In your mercy make good our lack of love,
so that we might be renewed by your generous grace.

117 You have no favourites, loving God;
this we have learned in Christ,
 who touched the leper,
 embraced the children,
 blessed the sinner on the cross,
 wept when Lazarus died
 and would not condemn Pilate.
Loving God,
forgive us for our shallow friendship:
 we love those who love us,
 we love those who live like us,
 who speak like us
 and walk along our road.
Jesus, Lord, forgive us and let your spirit renew us.

118 Thank you, healing God,
that Christ is the Way, Truth and Life for us:
 clearing our vision,
 lifting our hearts,
 healing our souls.

Thank you, healing God,
that in and through Christ
we see and know your love for the world:
 love without measure,
 love freely offered,
 love life-transforming.

Thank you, healing God,
in Jesus' name.

119 Lord our God, we thank you:
Out of chaos
 came creation.
Through the waters of destruction
 came the promise of peace.
In the calling of a nation
 your purpose was proclaimed.
In the painful words of prophets
 anguish led to new life.

And in the birth, life, death and rising of Jesus Christ,
   your purpose took flesh,
   and hope was born for us all,
   his death heralding the promise of life.
And now, in the healing and challenging presence of your Spirit,
   the ashes of destruction
   become the seed-bed of renewal.
Lord our God, we thank you.

120 We give you thanks that in your Heavenly City
the leaves of the trees are for the healing of the nations.
By them we are reminded of Christ and the shedding
of his life for the well-being of others;
that he was stripped bare unto death and buried
that life might forever rise.

As always, our hearts are full of gladness for those
who maintain your sacred task of healing:
   through ancient custom or modern science;
   through combatting the diseases of poverty and the sicknesses of affluence;
   through renewed relationships between individuals, communities or
      nations.

We give thanks for the strength and renewal
we discover within our own lives and our church communities;
for here we have come to know Christ and his rising among us.

121 For the doctors' skills
of looking and testing,
used to diagnose what is wrong.
Lord of all healing: **We thank you.**

For the nurses' skills
in technology and care,
used to carry out treatments.
Lord of all healing: **We thank you.**

For the paramedics' skills
at accidents and emergencies,
used to reassure, and limit damage.
Lord of all healing: **We thank you.**

For medical workers with wide-ranging skills
in hospitals and the community,
used to bring help, hope and comfort.
Lord of all healing: **We thank you.**

122 Loving God,
Thank you for Christ's light shed in the world,
 breaking into the darkness of our soul's winter,
 casting hope amidst despair
 and completing our joy.

Loving God,
Thank you for Christ's light shining not from afar,
 but amongst us:
 heralding a spiritual springtime
 of renewal and recommitment.

Loving God,
Thank you for Jesus Christ, our winter-sun Saviour:
 shedding light into the gloom of godlessness,
 warming hearts to the wonder and hope of the gospel
 and piercing minds with new insights of faith.

Thank you, Loving God,
in Jesus' name.

123 Lord God, we thank you for the Way of your love in the life of your Son:
 a love so clear, a life so dear; a pattern for our pilgrim purpose.
We thank you for the Truth we receive in the life of your Son:
 a truth so precious, so demanding; a guide in our pilgrim purpose.
We thank you for the Life we find in the life of your Son:
 a life so vibrant, so persuasive; a model in our pilgrim purpose.
Lord God, for the Way to follow,
the Truth for hungry hearts,
the Life for pilgrims,
and above all for Jesus,
we give you thanks.

124 Abraham and Sarah, Moses and Aaron,
Naomi and Ruth, David and Jonathan,
Joseph and Benjamin, Shadrach, Meshach and Abednego,
Andrew, Peter, James and John,
Paul and Luke, you and me.
Friends together who know God.

In the name of Jesus, our friend,
we give thanks for the friendships we have known and shared:
    for the friendship of people who, although different from us,
        have shared their love freely, without prejudice,
    for the friendship of people who have helped us through difficult times,
        when others have ignored us,
    for the friendship of people who, despite the cost to themselves,
        have wanted to befriend us.

We give thanks for the friendship of Jesus;
    for his comfort in times of sorrow,
    his presence in our loneliness,
    his peace in our distress
    and his forgiveness of our guilt.
Grateful for his all-embracing love,
may we make our friendships worthy of him who loves us.

125 Thank you for your friendship, Jesus.
Thank you for being with me in every experience of my life.
Thank you for physical support
    when my imperfect body reveals its imperfections.
Thank you for mental support
    when I struggle with new ideas and skills.
Thank you for emotional support
    when family and friends make demands on my love.
Thank you for spiritual support
    when my faith falters, and I fear the future.
Thank you that at the end of my earthly life
    your friendship will see me safely home
    and you will be there to greet me.

126 Jesus our Healer, hear our prayers for health and well-being. We are a people who pollute, destroy, corrupt and harm our world and our own life.
   Beaten, disregarded Christ, grant us your health.

For those men and women who have difficult and distorted lives that give pain most of the time, for those whose hope is for peace and comfort, rather than healing; for doctors, nurses and attendants who know how little they can do.
   Wounded, distorted Christ, give your own comfort.

For those gripped in the jaws of addiction, for whom the daily intake of drugs only tightens the grip and further destroys hope; for relatives who are impotent to help, and whose temptation is to collude.
   Oppressed Christ, share your strength which can persist in darkness.

For the men, women and children who suffer from wasting diseases, who watch their strength decline and their bodies grow weak before due time; for relatives whose love is as strong as ever but who can only watch in love.
   Enduring Christ, confer your silent perseverance.

For those caught within the blows, snares and pitfalls of twisted, loveless or exploiting relationships; for those unable or unwilling to risk loving, trusting or forgiving.
   . Betrayed, confused Christ, open us to what we dare not face.

For those women and men who have lived long and happy lives and whose bodies are worn out and tired, who long for release and would welcome the freedom of death.
   Returning Christ, give your peace for the journey which is to come.

127 Here gathered for worship, Gracious God,
we come heavy-laden.
We wish we travelled lighter,
but the baggage of care and concern weighs us down.
Care and concern for others,
and, in truth, for ourselves too.
And we hear those gracious words,
   'Come to me all you who labour and are heavy laden
   and I will give you rest',
and our hearts lift.

Here gathered for worship,
our offering is not praise alone:
it is our whole selves,
joys and sorrows too,
and all that bears on our hearts.
We trust that Christ completes joy
and heals sorrow,
and will give peace that defies circumstance and reason.
And so we pray for those in need right now:
weighed down with wearying care,
consumed by anxiety,
submerged in sadness;
all who need to know
the healing hand of Christ in their lives.
In his name we pray.

128 We pray with all our hearts that we, here, become the Church you wish – and order our life in the way that best lets us fulfil our calling to proclaim good news to hungry souls.

We pray for the wider world and all who are in particular need. Some we know personally, some only by report, but all in need of the loving support of prayer.

Bless those caught up in tragedy and despair.
Bless those engulfed in conflict and confusion.
Bless those debilitated by illness and sorrow.
Bless those saddened by loneliness and grief.
Bless those now dying.

For all these – far from us or near to us –
we pray your peace and comforting strength.
We pray that we may always know that in deepest need we meet Christ,
and in loving acts for others, they too meet our Lord.
So may we be channels of your grace.

129 Let us pray for families, laying the foundations of what their members will become. May the quality of their relationships be positive.

Let us pray for the work of nurseries, play-groups, schools, colleges and universities; for children and students and the staff who work in them. May we value the contribution they make to individual lives and the life of society.

Let us pray for adult learners; those still struggling to learn to read and those training to improve their skills.
May we all be ready to go on learning throughout our lives.

Let us pray for those who influence society – politicians, journalists and broadcasters.
May their control of information and power to shape opinions be for the good of all.

Let us pray for ourselves as we learn how to live the faith.
May the whole life of the Church encourage each one of us to grow in faith.

Jesus, teacher, help us to learn from you so that we can rightly be called disciples.

130 We bring to you the troubles of the world:
Pray for places of conflict, war, intolerance.
Lord Jesus, where there is hatred, bring your love.

We bring to you broken relationships and mistrust:
Pray for governments, unions, the rich and poor.
Lord Jesus, where there is injury, bring your pardon.

We bring to you the Church, here and throughout the world:
Pray for ministry, those who seek, guide, serve and pray.
Lord Jesus, where there is doubt, bring true faith.

We bring to you all human sorrow:
Pray for the bereaved, lonely, anxious.
Lord Jesus, where there is sadness, bring your joy.

We bring to you ourselves, our trials and temptations:
Leave silence for private prayer.
Lord Jesus, may we be channels of your peace and love.

Lord Jesus, bless us in your service.

131 We pray, Gracious God,
that the Church lives up to Jesus' teaching.
Let your Church be salt:
    savouring the taste of the 'bread of life' for hungry souls;
    spicing their expectation that the gospel changes lives;
    cutting through the ice of hearts hardened
        to hearing the truth of your love.

We pray for the world and for ourselves,
and for salt of an altogether different kind:
    to cut caustically into evil lives,
    to corrode false hope,
    to bite deep into sinful resolve,
    to burn pain into shameless hearts.

We pray for all people caught up in such urgent need:
    that they find an altogether different taste in their lives,
    an altogether more healing experience,
    the penetrative salt of the gospel's good news
    piercing their misery and bringing relief.
We pray in the name and for the sake of Jesus Christ.

132 Lord Jesus, you offered friendship to the many people you met:
Lovingly speaking to the prostitute, freeing her from the bonds of past
    behaviour;
Lovingly healing the sick;
Lovingly embracing the untouchable outcasts of society;
Lovingly drying the eyes of those who wept;
Lovingly sharing bereavement with friends who mourned;
Lovingly teaching your slow-to-learn disciples;
Lovingly preparing your followers for your death and separation;
Lovingly preparing a meal for your friends on the seashore;
Lovingly offering your life-giving Spirit to all who trust you.

Lord Jesus,
we bring before you the many today who long for unconditional friendship.
We pray for all who work to meet the needs of men, women and children,
that they may reveal your love through practical caring.

133 When we are hurt by word or act and we want to retaliate,
Lord Jesus: **Show us what friendship means.**

When we are faced by the hungry in our own country or abroad,
Lord Jesus: **Show us what friendship means.**

When we see the homeless on our streets and we do not know how to react,
Lord Jesus: **Show us what friendship means.**

When the cry of injustice batters our ears,
Lord Jesus: **Show us what friendship means.**

When discrimination based on age, sex, race or religion is revealed,
Lord Jesus: **Show us what friendship means.**

When the world's peace and harmony are shattered by fear or jealousy,
Lord Jesus: **Show us what friendship means.**

That we may play our part in sustaining and extending your Kingdom of
Love,
Lord Jesus: **Show us what friendship means.**

134 Gracious God,
you have lastingly shown us and the whole world
your measure of love in Jesus Christ.
Christ's outstretched arms on the Cross
stand so clearly as a symbol of your whole-heartedness towards us:
an offer of freedom from sin
for all who will turn to believe and find faith,
a promise of wholeness to broken souls.

As Christ wrestled with his mission,
setting his face to the tasks before him,
so we would commit ourselves to the pilgrim path
as Christ's followers,
our arms outstretched to those in need,
wholehearted disciples of our wholehearted Lord.
In Christ's name.

135   As in Christ, you came into the world
to bring light and peace,
kissing the earth with love, with hope, with life,
so we, loving God, would be messengers of light:
bringing warmth where the world is cold,
light where the world is dark,
and joy where the world is sad.
In Christ's name.

136   Jesus, you are for us the Christ who is the Tree of Life.
Your leaves are for the healing of all people.

Grant us this day to shelter in your shade,
that we may clearly see the things which lead to health and healing,
well-being and peace.

Grant us to eat of your fruit,
that we may be strong to work for the health of our communities.

Grant us the use of your branches,
that we may shelter the homeless, defend the weak
and discover creative work for unemployed hands.

Grant us the sweet perfume of your flower,
that in all our efforts we may never lose the wonder
and delight of your presence.

137 *'The treasure and the glory of God*
is seen in the face of the Christ.'

Almighty and Eternal God,
Creator, Redeemer, Inspirer,
you have not left us wondering endlessly
and wandering aimlessly
in our desire to know you.
In Jesus, your Son,
you have made yourself perfectly known.
In Christ we have treasure beyond compare:
for in him we see you.
In Christ we sense glory without measure:
for your fullness dwelt in him.
Through Christ we learn of you:
for we are drawn to know more and understand fully.
We commit ourselves to the quest
in Jesus' name.

138 Jesus, our master and friend,
we promise to follow your way,
seek your truth
and live by the example of your life.
Strengthen us by your love,
so that we may be faithful to our promise.

139 God, you loved the world so much that you gave your Son.
We will give ourselves in worship and service to you.
Bind us together in that fellowship of love
which unites us to you, our Father,
through the Son
and in the power of the Holy Spirit.

140 This we have known, Lord:

Love that is gentle, sensitive, sympathetic;

Love that is warm, caring, all-embracing;

Love that is clear-sighted, never fooled;

Love that condemns wrong, but not the wrong-doer;

Love that shares joys and sorrows, laughter and tears;

Love that can transform lives!

Such is the love at the heart of the friendship you offer.

As we accept it,

make it ours

in the friendship we offer to others.

141 Jesus,

if human frailty becomes a burden to us,

if sickness seizes us in mind or flesh,

if the pain of loved ones becomes more than we can bear:

Jesus, healer,

be our health.

Jesus,

if life's deep questions overpower us,

if ignorance leads on to prejudice and hate,

if human folly spoils the life that you have given:

Jesus, teacher,

be our wisdom.

Jesus,

if ever human friendship spoils and withers,

if loneliness becomes the daily path we tread,

if it should seem that violence is winning:

Jesus, friend,

be our companion.

Jesus:
Lord and Servant

142 Lord,
    in this holy place,
    at this holy time,
    we, your people made holy,
    acknowledge your Lordship:
        over your world,
        over your Church,
        over our lives.

    Lord, we are yours.
    We come in homage.
    We come in wonder.
    We come in trust,
    trusting that the presence
    of your life-giving Spirit
    will transform our act of worship
    into an offering worthy
    of the Lord of lords.

143 Lord our God,
    God of Abraham, Isaac and Jacob,
    God of a wandering people;
    Lord our God,
    Holy One of Israel,
    God of a settled nation;
    Lord our God,
    God whom Jesus called, 'Abba' – Daddy,
    God of close relationships;

Lord our God,
we call you to be with us,
trusting that all who call on the name of the Lord will be saved.
As we worship you, give us a sense of our worth,
that we might serve you without fear,
holy and righteous in your sight,
all the days of our lives.

144 We cannot invite you to our worship, Lord,
for you are always here before us.
We cannot take you into the world,
for you have gone there before us.
Wherever we are, you are there.
Wherever we fail to go, you are there.
So in every place and at any time
we have confidence to call out your name,
and know that you are present.
Here and now, in this chosen place,
we make our prayer:
Come, Lord Jesus, come
and be with us.

145 Lord our God, you are the Lord of past, present and future. Everything came
from the energy of your love, and all things find their real home in you.

We come to remember the stories of the past and make the history of the
people of faith a part of our story and the way we see your world.

We come to worship you in the present: singing, praying, learning. We find
you around us and within us. Your love is in the people we meet and
strengthens our support for each other.

Inspired by the past and strengthened by your presence, we dare to look to
the future with hope.

146 Lord, you are everywhere to be found; never hidden, always present.
You are within the bounding stars and galaxies,
in the turning earth and the vast universe,
in rolling seas and the stretch of calm waters.
The fresh surge of spring well knows you,
as does summer's delight,
the promise of autumn fruitfulness greets you,
as does brisk winter's depth.

We find you in the joy of human friendship;
in hands outstretched for gifts, given and received,
in the thrust of birth and the quietness of accepted death.
You sit with us in the security of the family table,
food lovingly prepared, gladly shared.
We find you truly in broken bread,
and wine outpoured
in Christian fellowship.
In gifts to the homeless;
food for the hungry;
protest for the deprived;
you are ever to be found.

You share in the debate and argument that searches for truth;
in reading, writing, and the Scriptures' search
in words of prayer and depths of silence.

And best of all,
we see you in a manger-child and questing youth;
hear you in spoken word by lakeside and mountain,
meet you in Upper Room and on Emmaus road,
in agony and joy,
in obedience and Gethsemane loss.

And miracle beyond our understanding;
you are in me, in him and her,
in stranger and friend, in age and youth.

Take away the veil that hides our eyes from you.
Forgive the sin that darkens our sight of you.
Heal the brokenness that shatters our picture of you.
Renew the loyalty, without which we lose the vision of you.

147   Gracious God,
we have proclaimed 'Jesus is Lord' with our lips
but we have not proclaimed it with our lives.

We have been afraid to follow the Lord of Life
down the path of self-giving love,
and have sought easier ways.
We have been reluctant to seek the Lord of Peace
in times of quiet and contemplation,
and have preferred busyness and distraction.
We have been slow to obey the Lord of lords,
deafened by the demands of the false idols
of materialism, success and self-interest.

We have proclaimed 'Jesus is Lord' with our lips
but we have not proclaimed it with our lives.
We are truly sorry and ask you, merciful God,
to forgive us, cleanse us and reinstate us,
that the Lordship of your Son, Jesus Christ,
might be made known through our renewed lives.

148   Lord Jesus Christ,
we confess that we want to be lord of our own lives;
    to do what we want, in our own way, for our own benefit.
We confess that we want to be lord of the Church;
    to worship in ways that please us,
    to hear a gospel that comforts and doesn't disturb,
    to organize activities which meet our personal needs.
We confess that we want to be lord of the world;
    to take as much as we can without giving back,
    to live in prosperity even at the cost of others' poverty.
But deep down we know better.
To make lords of ourselves,
we must deny your Lordship.
Forgive us, Lord Jesus.
Renew our attitudes and our actions
so that we recognize your Lordship in every part of life.

149 Shepherd Lord,
we have all strayed like sheep,
each of us going our own way.
We have held back from the flock,
so that we could not even hear your voice.
We have grasped equality with you,
when we ought obediently to have followed you.
We have made judgements about others,
even though we knew that they also belonged to you.
We thought we knew best,
even though the well-trod paths are so familiar to you.
Forgive us, Lord; find your lost sheep
and draw us back again.

150 Father God,
you gave us the example of Jesus;
he did not exploit his equality with you,
he emptied himself to become human,
humbled himself to be a servant
and washed his disciples' feet.
Lord, wash away the dust and grime of our lives.
Remove the grit of failures and the stains of past mistakes.
Refresh us, and call us your friends,
so that we may serve you
in newness of life.

151 Servant Lord,
a stable marked your entrance and your birth,
the world took little notice of your life,
a city in despair brought forth your tears.
Your war-horse was a donkey through the streets,
a bowl and towel the sign of kingly reign,
and on a villain's cross you died
before you lay within a borrowed tomb.

When we seek power and influence, status and renown,
remind us, Lord.
Servant Lord, remind us.

152 Lord God, thank you for Jesus,
come as one of us,
bringing afresh your love and forgiveness,
challenging us with a new pattern for our living.
Thank you for his conviction:
  that all the world should be at peace;
  that all people should grow to maturity;
  and all relationships find the freedom that comes from love.
Bring us to such commitment to his servant-lordship,
that our prayers become active reality in our daily lives.

153 Your power, Lord God,
is greater than anything we can imagine,
yet you do not overpower us;
you express your will in the person of Jesus,
and call us to follow.

154 Eternal One,
How dare we give you any name?

As father you enfold us in a mother's arms,
As lord you come to us as servant,
As spirit you appear in flesh,
As judge you plead our cause,
As comforter you chide us in our faults,
As guide you let us find our pilgrim way,
And as our friend you plead your loneliness.

How dare we give you any name;
Save 'Love'?

155 Manger and stable Lord,
you did not enter our world with trumpet flourish.
You came as a servant to be our Lord.
   As we seek to influence the world into which you came so gently,
   give us the spirit of servanthood,
   and show us the path of service.

Child on the knee Lord;
When your disciples assumed hierarchy, jostling for the best places in the Kingdom,
you pointed to a child as a sign of your purpose.
   As we take our place in the world of commerce, work and politics,
   give us the spirit of servanthood,
   and show us the path of service.

Donkey-riding Lord;
When generals entered the city, high-riding on stallions,
and armies measured their worth in stolen bounty,
you mounted a donkey, and asked for nothing save a simple welcome.
   As in cities and towns we seek to create communities that honour your name,
   give us the spirit of servanthood,
   and show us the path of service.

Bowl and towel Lord;
When your friends thought the welcome gesture might reduce their status,
you bent and washed their feet.
   As we meet each other in the Church you died to create,
   give us the spirit of servanthood,
   and show us the path of service.

Cross-carrying Lord;
When cynics despised the cross as a symbol of failure and shame,
you took the burden on to your own shoulders
and became both lord and servant in one act of risk-taking love.
   As we proclaim the meaning of life and the demise of death,
   give us the spirit of servanthood,
   and show us the path of service.

Resurrection Lord;
When your closest friends thought the final curtain had fallen on love and life,
you drew close to them at garden, beach and roadside.
   As we talk to the bereaved and comfort the dying,
   give us the spirit of servanthood,
   and show us the path of service.

156 Lord Jesus Christ,
    where strides the force of might and power,
    where arrogance scorns all it sees,
    where over-weening pride counts others' worth as nothing,
    and takes its half-formed thoughts as final truth;
        let gentleness reign.
    And also in us,
    where gossip eats away a reputation,
    where hasty words prevent the caring glance,
    where prejudice blinds eyes and hinders good relationships,
    and builds its barriers against the thought of love;
        let gentleness reign.

157 God of majesty and power, we long for the day when the rulers of this world bow down before you, seeking to serve their people according to your principles of justice and mercy and love.
Lord of the world, we will work for the coming of your Kingdom of peace.
Jesus is Lord!   **He is Lord of all!**

God of grace and love, we long for the day when, as your Church, we truly fulfil our calling, worshipping you in spirit and truth and giving ourselves in service to you, the world and one another.
Lord of the Church, we will live together in love and we will witness to the reality of your good news.
Jesus is Lord!   **He is Lord of all!**

God of forgiveness and encouragement, each one of us longs for the time when we can truly say, 'I am yours alone', when, free from sin, we are one with you.
Lord of our lives, we will continue to seek for you, listen to you, pray to you and live for you.
Jesus is Lord!   **He is Lord of all!**

158 Lord Christ, you rule over all. Supreme authority is yours.
God has placed all things under your feet.
What have we to offer you?
Yet you have called the Church to be your body in the world. You want to work through us – using our gifts, our skills and our love, and transforming them.
So we gladly commit ourselves – all that we have and all that we are – to you.
        (Based around Ephesians 1.21-23)

Mothering Sunday

159 Come, Mother God,
come as an enfolding,
nurturing presence.
Come as steadfast love
    to hold us.

Come, Mother God,
come as an enabling,
strengthening force.
Come as tough love
    to let us go.

Come, Mother God,
come as friend and comforter,
healing our wounds,
walking our way.
Come as wounded healer
    to make us whole.

160 Eternal God,
Creator,
we gather to praise.
Potter, moulding the clay of being,
breathing sense and awareness.
Parent, loving new life to birth,
bringing to fruit the seeds of existence.
Loving God, maker and minder,
we gather to praise.

Gracious God,
Redeemer,
we gather to praise.
Become flesh in Jesus, your Son,
nurturing your infant people,
ever forgiving, renewing, fulfilling.
Food and Drink for needy pilgrims,
we gather to praise.

Almighty God,
Inspirer,
we gather to praise.
Burning flame,
firing despairing disciples
to spread the gospel's good news;
Guide and Strength, carrying us on the Way to Truth,
we gather to praise.

One God, Father, Son and Spirit,
we gather to praise you.

161 Thank you, Loving God,
for all that you give to us
and all that you are for us.
Like a devoted mother,
you show patient mercy and gracious forgiveness:
    you give gifts for life,
    help us live to the full,
    and bring to the fore the fruits of your Spirit.
Thank you for mother-Church:
    nurturing our faith,
    feeding us milk when tender in years of faith,
    and meat as we grow to committed discipleship.
Thank you, Loving God,
    drawing us to the bosom of your care,
    embracing us with tender strength.
In Jesus' name we thankfully pray.

162 For the care of your Church, encircling God, we give you thanks.
In infancy we know its firm embrace, in childhood feel its gentle care,
as youth we hear its challenge and its urge.
Then with the growing strength of life, it gives us goals, ideals and hopes,
draws on our strength and shows us how to lean on others.
In older years, the challenge and the comfort are no less,
as still it takes, and gives, and calls, and trusts,
and all within the orbit of your care.

163 For the mothering of mothers
and the mothering of fathers;
for the mothering of others:
> **Mother God,**
> **we give you thanks.**

For those who act as midwife to our hopes,
for those who nurse us through our pain,
for those who nurture, strengthen and guide us:
> **Mother God,**
> **we give you thanks.**

For those who gently push us from the nest,
for those who welcome us home,
for those who become our family,
for the motherhood of the Church:
> **Mother God,**
> **we give you thanks.**

164 Loving God, we thank you for the grace of baptism:
> new life through death,
> a washing, a cleansing,
> a chance for renewal,
breaking the past, opening the future and fulfilling the present:
> like waters breaking to mould and mother us as we rise in the rite.

But not in baptism alone.
We die and rise endlessly in the turbulent waters of life.
We thank you that, by your Spirit,
> light ever dawns to banish darkness,
> the pathway forms through troubled waters,
> healing gifts absorb our pain
> and Lenten renewal brings your gracious forgiveness of our sin
> > leading us again to all that is good and right and true.
In Christ's name we give thanks.

165 Gracious God,
Father and Mother to us,
bathing us in compassion
and washing us from sin,
we rejoice in the hope of Lent,
and pray for those who are braving the flood:
   submerged in sorrow,
   drowned in despair,
   covered by guilt and shame.
We pray for all who feel themselves drifting:
   life's goals forgotten,
   life's hope un-renewed,
   life's purpose rootless,
      salvation seeming distant, or lost.
We pray for them in their fear and their sadness,
that they may re-emerge, healed and whole,
knowing themselves to be loved and valued by you.

We pray particularly
   for the grieving and the dying,
   the sick, and the lonely,
   the impoverished, and the outcast.
Bless them all with renewed courage, confidence and self-esteem,
   and a sense of belonging within your family.

Lord, flood them with love to strengthen and comfort them.

166 O Christ, our true mother,

   To mothering:
      to cradling and to nurturing,
      to holding and to letting go,
         We commit ourselves
         as your people
         in this place.

   To mothering:
      to comforting and to challenging,
      to forgiving and to releasing,
         We commit ourselves
         as your people
         in this place.

To mothering:
>to laughter and to friendship,
>to hospitality and to mission,
>>**We commit ourselves**
>>**as your community**
>>**in this place.**

167 Jesus, Lord of the Church, help us!
>Our doors are closed which should be open wide,
>our windows shadowed, keeping out the light,
>our roof, designed to shelter from the cold,
>>gives little comfort to the lost or sad,
>the notice-board proclaims events long dead,
>and passers-by see but an ancient tomb.

But in our folly and neglect
you do not leave your ailing Church.

Or so we think.

Father God, beget new life in us.
Mother God, re-birth your weakling child;
and take your Church where you would have it be:
>in street and road, in school and home,
>>to factory and pub, to screen and stage,
where you already live and work.
Restore obedience to your wasting Church
and point us to the glory of the Cross.

168 This we will do, Lord of the Church on earth:
>we will work till all the Church is one,
>strive until the Church finds needed strength,
>love as Christ has ever loved his Church,
>nurture the young as Christ took children on his knee,
>be prophet to a nation that ignores the truth,
>hold out a healing hand to every racial scar,
>and be as mother, father, friend,
>and thus become the Church of Christ.

Transfiguration to Calvary

Transfiguration

169 To make an act of worship,
we bring
ourselves:
    perhaps a little tired;
    perhaps a little preoccupied;
    expecting much, expecting little.
And we bring
our thoughts:
    some thankful and happy;
    some worried and anxious;
    some trivial, some deep.
And we bring
our words:
    the unexciting language of everyday;
    the difficult language of belief;
    the expressions of faith and fear, of doubt and hope.
All the ordinariness of our daily lives
we bring to this act of worship;
that with Christ we might climb
towards the mountain top to meet God
and find our human offerings
transfigured
by the glory of divine love.

170 The earth is full of your glory, Creator God:
the beauty of the natural world,
its order and design,
its intricacy and immensity,
its strength and delicacy;
the provision that is made
for humankind, for animals, for plants.
The earth is full of your glory, Creator God.

The Gospel is full of your glory, Son of God:
the beauty of your self-emptying love,
the holy child born in the stable,
the young man named by God at his baptism,
the man of sorrows hanging on the cross;
the gift of yourself for humankind,
in your teaching, your healing,
your dying for us and your rising again.
The Gospel is full of your glory, Son of God.

Your people are full of your glory, Holy Spirit:
the beauty of lives illumined by you,
loving hearts and willing hands,
brave followers and faithful friends,
peaceful souls and children of encouragement;
a people made one in you, whose lives shine out
like lamps in a dark world.
Your people are full of your glory, Holy Spirit.
Creator, Son and Holy Spirit, we praise you for your glory.

171 Mountain top and dreary plain,
Startling Presence and epileptic boy,
Depth of God-given truth and human questions,
Close companionship and solitary journey,
Success and failure, light and darkness –
All these are gifts, O God, if we will but see it:
resources of the Kingdom,
steps along the way,
moments of insight,
transfiguring our life, and work and hope.

172 Lord, the disciples glimpsed something of your glory on the mountain top;
the glory of God revealed to God's people
through the written word,
through the spoken word,
through Jesus Christ, the living Word.

Lord, you offer us glimpses of your glory;
in the world you have made,
through worship and prayer,
through other people.
But we confess, Lord, that, like those early disciples,
we do not know how to react.
We love the glimpses of your glory.
We long for spiritual 'highs'.
We would live with you on the mountain top of faith,
for we do not know how to reflect your glory
in our everyday lives on the plains.

Lord, forgive us for rarely allowing you to transfigure our lives
with the glory of your love.
Fill us with the light of your Spirit,
that in all our dealings with other people,
in all that we think and do and say,
your glory may be revealed.

173 God of light,
Light of light,
Light in our darkness,
Light to pierce even brightness,
Shine on us.
If truth is seen, then bless us.
If darkness, illuminate.
If sin, forgive.
If hope, renew
For Jesus' sake.

Palm Sunday

174 Where are you, God?

Are you in that temple with the golden dome?
Are you in the holiness of lamp and liturgy,
                sacrifice and psalm?
Are you in the sacred words of Moses and the prophets,
                of priests and wise men?
Are you in religion, rusty and ragged,
                established and empty?

Or are you in the heart and soul of Jesus,
        in his dusty feet
            and calm command,
    in his weeping over the city
        and his love of his nation,
    in his anger with the traders,
    in his fears of Judas' treachery,
    in his closeness to his friends
        and his worries for their future?

And are you here
as we remember the day when palms were waved
            and Hosannas sung
without any clue about what would happen?

God of Palm Sunday,
open our eyes and ears.
Speak to our needs,
        our hopes,
        our cities,
    we pray.

175 Loving God, this special day is here:
The turning point;
Heights of fame and fortune
Slide towards pain and death.
Exalted by the humility of a donkey
And the cheers of children,
Crowds shout 'Hosanna'.
Had we been there
We would have joined in the roar of praise,
Lifted hearts and voices,
Exclaimed 'Hosanna'.

And then so soon; only days;
The crowds bayed
Like a pack of wolves
For your blood.
Had we been there
We confess, Lord,
We would have joined them,
Cursing when we should have praised.

So we come,
Humbly,
Hands empty,
Awaiting the darkness of Friday,
And beyond,

To the light of Easter.
Take our faithlessness,
Wipe it clean and lead us on,
With hands that weep spots of blood
Onto our own,
Because of your love.

176 'Hosanna, hosanna, hosanna in the highest!
Blessed is he who comes in the name of the Lord.'

Lord, with the people of Jerusalem,
and with Christians the whole world over,
we acclaim you as our King.

If we had been there that morning;
    we would have spread our cloaks at your feet,
    waved our palm branches over your head,
    worshipped you as the Messiah.

As we worship you this morning;
    we offer ourselves in your service,
    we adore you with our whole heart,
    we worship you as our Saviour.

177 Hosanna, Son of David!
We greet you
as the fulfilment of all our hopes.

You alone hold the keys of the Kingdom.
You alone can show the world
    how leaders ought to lead,
    how kings ought to rule,
    how power ought to be exercised,
    how politicians ought to serve,
    how priests ought to minister,
    how ordinary people can be saints,
    how donkeys can pull royal coaches.

You are worthy of honour and power,
yet you come to us in humility and meekness;
you deserve worship and glory
yet it's the last thing you ask for.

Accept our hosannas this day.
May they be accompanied
by lives of obedience to your way
and deeds of service and reconciliation
in your name.

178 We cannot keep silent.
For all the great things you have done in Jesus,
    wonderful God,   **we praise and adore you.**
For his charismatic presence,
    wonderful God,   **we praise and adore you.**
For his humility,
    wonderful God,   **we praise and adore you.**
For his love for the people,
    wonderful God,   **we praise and adore you.**
For all that we know from the Bible stories,
    wonderful God,   **we praise and adore you.**
For his obedience even to death on the cross,
    wonderful God,   **we praise and adore you.**
For his glorious resurrection,
    wonderful God,   **we praise and adore you.**
For opening the way to heaven for us,
    wonderful God,   **we praise and adore you.**
We have to shout out
because we have witnessed your love
revealed in your Son Jesus Christ,
    wonderful God,   **we praise and adore you.**

179 This Palm Sunday,
help us to hold to your idea of kingship
which is still ridiculed by the powerful
and scorned by the successful.

Let the picture of a king on a donkey
be hung in every leader's gallery;
        every politician's office;
        every scholar's library;
        every minister's study;
and seen in every disciple's life.

180 Merciful God,
today we are reminded
of human fickleness.
We cry 'Hosanna' one minute and 'Death' the next.
We are a hot and cold humanity;
unreliable and selfish.
We have allowed Good Friday to be repeated
throughout the generations
and across the centuries;
refusing to see clearly
the meaning and message of Palm Sunday.

Forgive us
for our hollow 'Hosannas';
for seeking a God to match
    our national dreams and private goals;
for failing to look into Jesus' eyes
    or understand his mind and heart;
for persisting in our worship
    of narrow horizons and exclusive attitudes.

Ride into our tired lives,
turn over our tables of prejudice,
put to flight our doves of deceit,
and help us to build our lives
        as cities of love
        and temples of justice,
pointing to your Kingdom of liberation and joy.

181 *Jesus wept over the city of Jerusalem.*

God, do you weep over us
because we have not understood
nor accepted your Son as our Lord?
Do you despair of us,
that we shall never find the way that leads to peace
but always end up in conflict?
Do you wonder when we will learn
to follow the teachings of Jesus
and live in harmony?

We know the answer:
we still cause you to weep.
Forgive us, Lord.

Jesus drove the traders out of the temple.

God, do we still ruin your house of prayer
with our concern for the material
and not the spiritual things of life?
Do we still need you to drive out the evil within us
and make us clean?
Do we still seek to do away with you,
if not by our deliberate actions,
at least by our apathy?

We know the answer:
sin still abounds.
Forgive us, Lord.

Jesus gave his life on the cross for us.

God, forgive us for the sin
of ignoring your ways
and failing to live according to your commands.
We ask it in the name of your Son, our Saviour, Jesus Christ.

182 God of Jerusalem,
of cities beautiful and violent,
of palm trees and children and donkeys;
God of Jesus, of Mary, of Peter,
of Pilate and Judas and Barabbas;
how can we put into words
our praise and admiration
for the meaning of this day
as it speaks to us and the world?

You have given to us an eternal sign
that a man on a donkey
can transform history
and demonstrate to every city and every government
that peace is the only possible goal for creation.
   You have put to flight
   the idea that strength relies on violence.
      You have dispelled the notion
      that kingdoms need to be founded on fear.

You have given the lie
to intrigue, deceit, religious arrogance,
naked nationalism, and force of arms.
   You have displayed to us and all people
   that the only king in whom we can truly rejoice
   is the one who comes to us in the name of the Lord;
   the one whose way is non-violence,
   and the one whose heart is full of compassion
   for the downtrodden and oppressed.

Thank you for the good news of this day:
that the king whom you bring to us is a servant,
and the judge whom you offer to us is a redeemer.

Thank you for all those
in authority and leadership across the world
who glimpse this vision and build their kingdoms upon it.

Thank you also for ordinary people
who are engaged in the struggle for peace
and who refuse to give up.
Bless all peacemakers who come in the name of the Lord.
We ask it in the name of Jesus, Prince of Peace.

183 We give thanks that your wisdom is greater than ours.
Your Son turned the world upside-down
and challenged the ways of human beings with divine grace.

He rode on a donkey, although he came as a King.
He went to the poor, although he was the Lord.
He healed the sick, although accused of breaking the Law.
He died on a cross, although he had never sinned.
He rose again, overcoming human death with eternal life.

We give thanks that your love is greater than ours.
Your Son was greeted as the Messiah,
yet soon after was rejected and reviled by the very same people.

In love he guided the disciples, to prepare them for the future.
In love he entered the city and the Temple.
In love he shared his knowledge of you, his Father.
In love he took the way of the Cross.
In love he did not condemn even those who crucified him.

All these things fill us with wonder.
They seem in such contrast to the ways of the world, to our ways.
We can only give thanks that they were your ways.
Thanks be to God, who continues to surprise us.

184 *'The Master needs it.'*

Lord, we commit ourselves to you;
    call us as your disciples and we will follow you,
    say go and we will go,
    tell us what to do and we will do it,
    give us the words and we will speak them.
Master, we seek only to serve you and to know your will for us.
Fill us with the confidence and faith to obey your call
and to answer your challenges,
so that we may show our love for you.
Because you, our Lord, were obedient to the end.

185 Gracious God,
    let the stones cry out
    and the trees clap their hands
    if we fail to offer Jesus a royal welcome today.
    If our arms are not raised to wave,
    if our voices are not shouting 'Hosanna',
    if our hearts are not moved to respond with joy,
    then let the pavements ring
    and the city squares resound with thanksgiving.

    Bring from our stuttering discipleship
    a new consistency,
    so that we are committed to Jesus' way
    with a passion and enthusiasm
    which does not pass like early morning mist,
    but holds strong in the face of opposition and failure.

    As this unholy week unfolds
    and we remember how Jesus was left friendless,
    help us to recognize those moments when and situations where
    we become betrayers,
    resort to denial
    and run away, leaving Jesus alone.

        May your Spirit
        strengthen and support us,
        so that we are given courage and conviction
        when justice is challenged and peace endangered.

        May your Spirit
        provide us with silence or words
        to combat the taunts of the godless
        and the prejudice of the religious.

        May your Spirit
        console and comfort us
        if we find ourselves isolated and maligned
        for championing the powerless
        or sharing the pain of the defeated.

    Gracious God,
    we will walk with the donkey
    and hold to your idea of kingship.

186   Merciful God, forgive
         that we fall asleep
         when you call us to watch and pray.
         We fail to see the signs of your coming.

      Christ our Saviour, forgive
         that we are not watchful.
         We do not choose hope
         or plant the seeds of hopefulness.
         We fail to see the signs of your coming.

             God over all,
             Christ within us,
             Spirit around us,
             hear our prayer
             and send your messenger
             of peace to us and to your sleeping world.

187   Cross-carrying Jesus,
      as you stagger on your lonely journey,
      time slips,
      worlds reel.
      Forgive us that we turn away,
      embarrassed,
      uncaring,
      despairing.
      Help us to stay with you through the
          dark night;
      to watch and wait;
      to know the depths of your anguish
      and to realize that you carry us,
      forgiven – even us,
      and love us.
         Forgive us,
         that we get on with our work unthinking,
         that we gamble unknowing with precious things.

      Cross-carrying Jesus,
      nailed to the tree of life,
      forgive us
      and grant us your salvation.

Good Friday

188 Today is a solemn day.
The day when we remember
the sufferings and death
of Christ our Lord upon the cross:
the total self-giving of Love
for the beloved
in pain, in humiliation, in despair.

Lord, as we worship you this day,
fill us with wonder,
with gratitude,
with solemn joy,
in the name of our crucified Messiah,
our uplifted Saviour, Jesus Christ.

189 Jesus, stand among us
as the silent one who forbore to argue your own case.
Strengthened by your stillness, may we refrain from rushing into self-defence.

Jesus, stand among us
as the ridiculed one who would not condemn your persecutors.
Made wise by your foolishness, may we accept mockery with good grace.

Jesus stand among us
as the vulnerable one who would not save yourself from death.
Healed by your brokenness, may we take up the cross of the outcast.

190 Creator God, you are almighty, powerful,
the Maker of heaven and earth,
the sovereign Lord of all – yet
you love us more tenderly than a mother or father,
more wholeheartedly than a partner or friend.
The immensity of your love astounds us.
Creator God, we worship you.

Son of God, you are the eternal Word,
the majestic Messiah, Christ the King – yet
emptying yourself of all but love,
you gave yourself up to humankind,
made of yourself a precious gift
which could be rejected, mocked, destroyed.
The immensity of your love astounds us.
Son of God, we worship you.

Holy Spirit, you are the creative breath of God,
roaring wind and flames of fire,
the mighty Lord of Life – yet
you enter our lives with gentleness,
you fill us with peace and hope,
with courage and faith and joy.
The immensity of your love astounds us.
Holy Spirit, we worship you.

191 God, who clothes the earth with rich and beautiful garments;
we adore you in the austere nakedness of the man on the cross.

God, who acts with passion and love in the history of the world;
we adore you in the waiting stillness of the man on the cross.

God, who claims all in heaven and on earth for your commonwealth;
we adore you in the self-abandonment of the man on the cross.

192 O God, we confess that when our ease is threatened
or anything we hold dear is put at risk,
we run away in fear.

When darkness covers the land
and the curtain of the temple is torn in two,
Lighten our clouded minds,
heal our divided hearts
and forgive our putting goodness to death.

O God, we confess that while great injustices are perpetrated around us,
we throw dice and embrace trivialities.

When darkness covers the land
and the curtain of the temple is torn in two,
Lighten our clouded minds,
heal our divided hearts
and forgive our putting goodness to death.

O God, we confess that while the wounded of the earth cry out in agony,
we noisily justify our inaction
and do not listen to their pain.

When darkness covers the land
and the curtain of the temple is torn in two,
Lighten our clouded minds,
heal our divided hearts
and forgive our putting goodness to death.

Hear the word of forgiveness.

Here is hope:

When we admit what we are,

the light of the world overcomes our darkness;

the good physician heals our dividedness.

And whether we admit this or not;

the Christ once crucified is risen

and works within us.

193 Loving Parent God,
     when we think of all that you have done for us;
        in the giving of your Son to be our teacher, healer and friend,
        and to become our crucified Saviour,
     we realize with great sorrow how poor are the gifts we offer to you.
     Our praise is short-lived and distracted.
     Our lives are often obsessed by things of little importance.
     Our loving is limited and tainted by mixed motives.

     You have shown us, in Christ, that yours is the love that gives all,
     even to dying for our sins.
     We ask you to forgive us,
     strengthen and enrich us
     with your Holy Spirit,
     so that we may truly live for you
     in the name of our Crucified Saviour.

194 For creating all that is;
     the universe in its splendour,
     the world in its beauty and diversity,
         Loving God: **We thank you.**
     For creating the human race to live in relationship with you and one another,
         Loving God: **We thank you.**
     For giving us the freedom to choose between good and evil,
     the freedom to respond to you in thanks and love,
         Loving God: **We thank you.**
     For not forsaking us when we choose to turn our backs on you,
         Loving God: **We thank you.**
     For sending us your son, Jesus Christ, to show us the way to Life,
         Loving God: **We thank you.**
     For sending us your son, Jesus Christ,
     who, by his dying on the cross,
     revealed the depth of your forgiving love for us,
         Loving God: **We thank you.**
     As we remember the death of Jesus,
     our hearts are full of gratitude for such a love
     freely given,
     not counting the cost,
     poured out for all.
     Saving God, we praise and thank you.

195 Thank you, gentle God ...
Thank you?
Did I really say 'Thank you'?
Thank you for plaited thorns, scourging, spitting and jeering?
Thank you for the nakedness, the piercing, the bleeding?
Thank you for that sense of abandonment, those racking breaths,
    that blackness?
Thank you for all this?

Thank you, gentle God ...
Thank you?
Did I really say 'Thank you'?
Thank you for the internment camp,
    the torturer's instruments, the stinking prison cell?
Thank you for this twisted limb, that damaged brain, these wounded hearts?
Thank you for abuse, terror, disease, bereavement, despair?
Thank you for all that?

Yes, thank you!
Thank you for being there
at the very heart of it all.
Not the perpetrator,
but the recipient of the cruelty,
suffering with each one who suffers,
alongside, and at one with us all.

196 **'Do this to remember me' – a eucharistic prayer**

We remember as opposed to forgetting.
We re-member to heal dismemberment, partition, breaking.

Christ, bridge between past and future,
we thank you as we recall your death.
Body broken, blood shed,
breath extinguished: crucified
because you would not compromise
your integrity, vision, compassion –
because you would not turn away
from the poor, the oppressed, the outcast,
but must be there on the edge, with them to the end.
This we remember for tomorrow's sake.

Christ, bridge between divine and human,
we thank you as we recall your death.
Body broken, blood shed, here in stark reminders
of the scandal of your incarnation
by which you re-membered and connected once again
heaven and earth, spiritual and material, soul and body –
hallowing bread and wine, and humankind, and the land ...
broken, poured out, you re-member us,
Easter re-members you – for life's sake.

197 Lord,
in Jesus
you gave everything for us.
He embraced the limitations of human life,
accepting the risks, the self-surrender, the pain of love;
the Son of God
became the Man for Us.
His perfect loving
brought him to the Cross,
for we found such loving
too much to accept.

Lord,
help us not to reject you
and your love,
even though it is hard to grasp
the enormity of the gift of yourself.

Lord, you are our God.
We are your people.
Pour your love into our lives,
that we, too, may be able to give all
for you, for one another, for the world,
for the sake of our crucified Saviour,
Jesus Christ the Lord.

198 'Lord Jesus Christ,
you became poor,
that through your poverty
we might become rich.'

Thus enriched,
we shall not be afraid to become poor again:
    poor as we sit light to possessions;
    poor as we refuse privilege and share power;
    poor as we identify with the downtrodden;
    poor as we give away our time to others;
    poor as we bear ridicule for the stand we take;
    poor as we shed masks and accept our vulnerability;
    poor as we carry our aloneness with courage;
    poor as we acknowledge our not-having, our not-knowing;
    poor as we walk the way of the cross;
    poor as we surrender our lives to God.

We shall not be afraid to die, in Christ,
to our obsession with self, our prejudice, our greed,
for in such dying
we richly live.

We praise you for this assurance of life
given through the death of Jesus –
treasure beyond price.

Easter

199 We have waited;
we waited quietly for this day,
this Rising Day overflowing with hope.
And Christ has risen.

We have waited;
we waited patiently for this day sustained by trust;
for all our folly and shallow wisdom
we still have faith in God.
And Christ has risen.

We have waited;
we waited earnestly for this day, sustained by anger;
for we know just how much this world
is in need of a new start.
And Christ has risen.

200 Now the picture is complete,
now the story is fully told.
The jigsaw is finished:
the trinity of grace –
the cradle, the cross, the rising –
dovetail together.
The cradle of the birthing:
    our God come amongst us,
    in flesh to share the life we lead.
The cross of sacrifice:
    our God loving us to death.
The rising of hope:
    our God embracing us to eternity.
Our new day rises in resurrection light,
the long wilderness walk of Lent behind,
the darkness of the Cross ended.
We approach you now, loving God,
with renewed joy in our song,
and strengthened hope in our hearts.
We worship, in the name and for the sake of our living Lord,
Jesus Christ.

201 Gracious and Eternal God,
our hearts lift with the moment of this morning.
Now we see more clearly the way,
now we know more nearly the truth,
now we find more dearly the life.
This is the day of rising.
This is the day of unutterable joy.
This is the day of death's defeat.
This is the day you have made new
 all our dearest desires,
 all our hopes and schemes and dreams,
 all our chances to choose
 to live for the sake of our risen Lord Jesus Christ.
This is the day, and this is the time,
today, now we gather before you in worship,
in the name of the same Lord Jesus Christ.

202 A familiar figure on a distant shore,
A familiar action at a kitchen table,
A presence in the midst of doubt,
O Risen Christ,
You come to surprise us and delight us,
You open wide the door to joy.
Hopeful, we worship you.
Hesitant, we adore.

203 This is the day that starts a week.
This is the day of rising.
This is the day that starts new life.
This is the day to sing for joy.
For Christ our Lord, though killed on a Cross,
is now alive for ever.

And so we gather, to rejoice and give thanks
that this day and all our days
are lived in the light of that hope.
In the name of Jesus, Christ our Lord.

204 Loving God,
the depth and breadth and cost of your love is now known.

In the birth of Jesus,
heaven and earth fuse in a child:
you draw back the veil of separation,
and touch the temporal with the eternal.
Christ lays aside the divine cloak,
and takes instead the mantle of a slave.
Loving God, we worship you.

In the death of Jesus your Son,
our sin and your grace embrace:
you cast light into the darkness of our deeds,
and offer the hand of forgiveness to us.
Christ lays down his life for our sakes,
and takes our place on the cursed Cross.
Gracious God, we worship you.

In the resurrection of Jesus,
the treasure of renewal is seen,
the breaking of despair's spiral known,
and assurance for the future found.
Christ rises again to life,
and hearts lift from the depth of sorrow.
Eternal God, we worship you.

205 This is your day, eternal Lord:
yours by right of death and resurrection,
yours by victory over cross and grave,
yours by the triumph of unbounded love.

And in your mercy you have made it our day:
ours by your gift,
ours as your love stoops down to meet us,
ours as we reach up in love to you.

Yours and ours; Easter Day.
You are our Lord; we are your people.
Thanks be to God.

206 Loving God,
we sing to you with cheerful voice,
and come before you and rejoice,
for now we know that you are God, indeed:
maker of all, through and through creation.
> We praise and adore you.

Loving God,
entering our humanity in Jesus,
living as us,
dying for us,
rising to life to confirm Easter's hope for the world.
> We praise and adore you.

Loving God,
powerfully present in your Spirit,
drawing us to truth,
guiding us to light,
showing us the Way, Truth and Life for all time.
> We praise and adore you.

Father, Son and Spirit,
one God, for ever and ever.
> We praise and adore you.

207 We breathe easy today,
as we celebrate Christ's rising.
Today is joy, today is light,
today is breezy, bubbly, unfettered festivity.
Today is life, Gracious God,
and our hearts are fit to burst with delight.

Forgive us our partial view.
Forgive us for fleeing to the Rising,
and running past the Cross.
Forgive us for failing
to take the time and pay the cost
of waiting at the foot
of the rustic gallows,
while the price of love was borne for us.

Like the disciples, we desert all too quickly:
horrified and fearful.
Forgive us, Gracious God,
and free us to celebrate with deeper understanding
that our joy has been bought at great price
by Christ, in whose name we pray.

208 Lord of the morning,
we come in shame and in fear.
Our lives are imprisoned by false expectations.
We have walled ourselves up
with lies and half-truths.
We are trapped, fearful and ashamed.
Who will roll the stone away?

Lord of Creation,
we come in shame and in despair.
The delicate balance of your creation
has been destroyed.
The fragile face of the earth is mutilated.
We are trapped by the demands of our greed.
Who will roll the stone away?

The God who walked in the garden,
The Christ mistaken for a gardener,
The Spirit who nurtures growth,
will roll away the stones
that choke the life of the planet.
The three in one
will roll away the boulders
that imprison us in guilt.
God will roll the stone away!

When we, grieving,
confess;
when we, forgiven,
work for truth and peace;
God will release us
from the tomb
of our despair.

209 Our hearts lift to give you thanks, our God of new beginnings.
From the beginning of Creation onwards, you have been bringing newness to be, causing chaos to be turned to order, darkness to light, and barrenness to life. Today of all days, we remember the fundamental newness you give to the world through the resurrection of Jesus Christ from the dead: the new beginning of all time, the hope for us all.

The resurrection is dawn to the Cross's night,
life to the Cross's death,
healing to the Cross's hurt,
embrace to the Cross's forsakenness,
hope to the Cross's despair.
All is new, God of new beginnings,
our hearts lift to give you thanks.

210 Thanks be to you, loving God,
for the joy at the heart of the faith we profess:
a joy not built on the sand of whim and fancy,
but on the rock of Christ.

Thanks be to you, loving God,
for the gospel's utterly good news,
timelessly relevant all times, everywhere.

Thanks be to you, loving God,
for the sure anchor to our ships that faith can give.
Buffeted by the storms and swept by tides,
still we are not wrecked, still we do not sink,
still we can ride out the tempest.

Thanks be to you, loving God,
for the utter joy of Easter,
death and darkness overcome by life and light:
the pain of the Cross swallowed up
in the dawn hope of resurrection.

Thanks be to you, loving God,
for the power and passion of the gospel:
to transform, and complete, and make new,
in Jesus' name.

211 On this rising day:
We give thanks for the memory of those women
who travelled early to the tomb,
who, although forsaken beyond belief,
did not desert the stricken Christ,
and who became the first ones to glimpse
the miracle of a universe restored.
Therefore,   **we cry aloud Hallelujah!**

We remember those men,
the close companions of the new revelation;
for whom closeness to Jesus
was both binding and blinding,
but who were not rejected for such frailty.
Therefore,   **we cry aloud Hallelujah!**

We remember women and men of every generation
who have borne testimony to life springing from the dead;
to grief as the harbinger of new beginnings.
Therefore,   **we cry aloud Hallelujah!**

We remember that parents have lived in poverty,
and raised children, yet never abandoned hope,
exampling for their young the way of Christ.
Therefore,   **we cry aloud Hallelujah!**

We remember those pioneers who believed in what they could not see
and who refused to allow hardship or opposition to deter them.
Therefore,   **we cry aloud Hallelujah!**

We remember those men and women who have lived within the maelstrom
of political and economic change
and have not given their soul as the price of a vote.
Therefore,   **we cry aloud Hallelujah!**

We remember those who lived outside of their times,
who have seen their vision trampled upon,
or whose labours of love have been dismantled,
but who have kept faith in themselves.
Therefore,   **we cry aloud Hallelujah!**

212 Risen Christ,
for recognizing you
in the Scriptures;
for recognizing you
in the breaking of bread;
for finding you in the stranger:
    We give you thanks.

Risen Christ,
for times of doubt and struggle,
for times of confusion and chaos,
for times of wrestling for a blessing:
    We give you thanks.

For thankfully
you are present
in bread and in battle,
in darkness and in doubt,
in every corner of our lives,
in every place in our world,
for you have gone before us.

Send us out
with thankful hearts
to live and work
in your name
and to your glory.

213 If we should not rejoice this day,
And give you thanks, Lord Jesus Christ,
Let the stone roll back and seal the tomb again.
Let Mary, sorrow-laden, stumble from the morning garden.
Let Cleopas eat bread with tears, the Christ unrecognized.
Let Thomas hold his doubt as truth,
And Peter keep denial unforgiven.

But no,
The truth is out, and death has died.
The earth is bathed in resurrection light,
And we give thanks, rejoicingly.

214 Bless to us, O God, this day, fresh made.
In the chorus of birds – bless us.
In the scent of blossom – bless us.
In the wet grass and the spring flowers – bless us.
Bless us and heal us,
for we come to you in love and in trust.
We come to you in expectant hope:

    Silence

O God, give us a well of tears
to wash away the hurts of our lives.
O God, give us a well of tears
to cleanse the wounds,
to bathe the battered face
of our world.
O God, give us a well of tears
or we are left, like arid earth,
unsanctified.

    Silence

Heal us and your grieving world
of all that harms us.
By the power of your Resurrection
restore us to new life,
set us on new paths,
bring us from darkness to light,
help us to choose Hope.

Jesus says, 'Pick up your bed and walk':
pick up the bed of your sorrows and fears,
pick up the bed of your grief and your sin,
pick up your life and come, come follow Him.

215 Jesus of the Emmaus Road,
Come as we walk the lonely path, and be our companion.
Come when life mystifies and perplexes.
Come into our disappointments and unease.
Come at table where we share bread and hope,
and coming, open our eyes to recognize you.

216 Let there be an up-rising
of Christ – crushed, crucified, entombed.
Let the earth crack!
Let stones be rolled away!
Let the dawn push back the blanket of the night!
Let the trumpets sound!
Let flowers open!
For we welcome the One who affirms life!

Let there be an up-rising
of God's little ones – dispossessed, outcast, silenced.
Let their land be given back to them!
Let the stones blocking their liberty be rolled away!
Let their stubborn hopes for tomorrow re-shape
the dark realities of today!
Let their own stories be heard!
Let our ears and hearts be opened to them!
For their struggles reveal the One who affirms life!

(This prayer was prompted by Kenith A. David's *Sacrament and Struggle*, W.C.C.)

217 Risen Lord,
yours is the power that reaches every human heart.
You understand our ways,
you speak to us in both our sorrow and our joy,
you match your step to ours, and lead us on.

Risen Lord,
yours is the power that sweeps throughout the Church.
You come to bless us and to judge,
you come in compassion and in challenge,
you come to affirm, and come to change our foolish ways.

Risen Lord,
yours is the power that stretches to the ends of the earth.
You span the nations in your glory and your power,
you hear the call of every tongue,
you live within the swirling cultures of our time.
Risen Lord, come with power this Easter Day.
Touch hearts, and lives, and every church,
and make the kingdoms of this world, the Kingdom of our God.

218 *'Unless I see the mark of the nails on his hands, unless I put my finger into the place where the nails were, and my hand into his side, I will never believe it.'*

John 20. 25

Put your hand,
Thomas,
on the crawling head
of a child
imprisoned
in a cot
in Romania.
Place your finger,
Thomas,
on the list of those
who have disappeared
in Chile.
Stroke the cheek,
Thomas,
of the little girl
sold into prostitution
in Thailand.
Touch, Thomas,
the gaping wounds
of my world.
Feel, Thomas
the primal wound
of my people.
Reach out your hands,
Thomas,
and place them at the side of the poor.
Grasp my hands, Thomas,
and believe.

This prayer can be altered to respond to changing world-wide political situations.

219   Loving God, we rejoice in the hope that is at the heart of Easter:
    the rising, the new beginning,
    the light of resurrection flooding over the shadow of the Cross.
We pray for the Church:
that we may live and speak as people of the resurrection,
    showing by our words and deeds
    the sense of joy and purpose that Easter brings.
But we are too well aware
that the light of the resurrection is obscured from many
by the deep darkness of their shadowland existence.
We pray for those bowed low by the weight of sorrow and despair
    through illness or bereavement,
    through loss of self-confidence, guilt, shame or fear.
We pray for those caught in the cross-fire of conflicts
    and fearing for their future.
We pray for those who feel hope snatched from them by sad circumstance.
For all such, we pray that their shadows
be pierced by resurrection light,
and hope spring newly eternal within them.

220   The tale is told, the deed was done,
the Christ was killed, but rose again.
And now we know the words to say,
Christ is the truth, the life, the way.

    Eternal God,
    we commit ourselves to that way,
    we crave that life,
    we hunger after that truth.

    We pray our days
    are touched by both
    cross-shadow and resurrection-light:
        the love and hope
        at the base of our belief,
        the pain and purpose
        at the root of our faith,
        the cost and gift
        at the heart of our calling.
        In Christ's name.

221   Christ our risen Lord is our bread of life and our cup of salvation. We eat and drink of him in prayer, praise and communion: foretasting the feast of heaven and hearing again the promise of eternity. We pray that as we are sustained, so we will find words of life and ways of salvation to speak and live: that others who are hungry in the spiritual desert of sorrow and doubt may know peace and light in their lives. In Christ's name we pray.

222   To you, O God,

who has led us out of captivity,

through the wilderness,

into the garden of Gethsemane

and to the cross,

we cling.

To you, O God,

who has led us out of captivity,

through the wilderness,

into the garden of burial

and to an empty tomb,

we cling.

O Risen Christ,

unclasp our clinging hands.

Turn us from death to life,

and as we commit ourselves

anew to you,

send us out

to tell others

the good news

of your Easter.

Ascension, Pentecost and Trinity

Ascension

223 Ascending Christ, returning to your beginning,
you take the joy and anguish of human struggle
into the presence of God.
Intercede for us this day, that the breath of God
may fill the emptiness you leave among us
and we may sense the glory which now is yours.

224 Our Lord has returned to his throne in heaven.
He is seen no more on earth.
Yet he lives
and is with us now and for all eternity.
We are in the presence of our ascended Lord.
We celebrate the mystery of our glorious King.

225 Jesus is seen in earthly form no more.
He is King of Kings: **And Lord of Lords!**

The risen Christ is ascended into heaven.
He is King of Kings: **And Lord of Lords!**

He sits at the right hand of God the Father.
He is King of Kings: **And Lord of Lords!**

Yet he has promised his Spirit will be with us on earth.
He is King of Kings: **And Lord of Lords!**

Let us rejoice and praise him, for
He is King of Kings: **And Lord of Lords!**

Now and for ever.
He is King of Kings: **And Lord of Lords!**

226 Playful God, you love us and draw close to us,
but you do not crowd us;
you allow us to weep, but provide us with joy;
you insist we follow, but disappear from sight.

We demand certainty, and you ask that we simply follow.
The child in our hearts adores the way you are.

You revealed yourself in Jesus and we were glad;
you hung him on the cross; we could not believe it;
you gave him to the world of the dead; we were beyond comfort;
you raised him to life; it was beyond belief.

We wonder at your love; our brokenness
adores the depth of your purpose.

Jesus, you fed your friends on the beach and they were happy again;
you appeared in unexpected places; they grew to accept it,
but then your goodbye was final;
you said go back to the starting place and all would be well.
And it was true!

Jesus, gone but present, comrade for ever,
through our friendship we adore your Father:
the dreamer, the planner, the lover without end.
We celebrate the glory which now is yours.

227 Lord, it is hard to understand why you had to leave your friends. Even though the disciples did not always succeed, it must have been easier to live by your teaching when you were present with them in human form.
You call us now to live by faith, but our faith is a fragile thing, weak and wavering.
Ascended Lord,
sometimes it is as though you have left us all over again.
Where are you:
    when children are starving,
    when the elderly are attacked in their homes,
    when governments fail to care for our nations' health and education,
    when the Church ignores even its most obvious tasks,
    when we fear the way of our dying and even death itself?

Yet by your resurrection you conquered death.
By your ascension, you offered us the glory of heaven.
By your Spirit, you offer to lead and guide us.
Forgive our lack of faith
and grant us that peace which holds faith firm in all circumstances.

228 Faithful God, you continue with us through the times
of parting, breaking and abandonment,
you are the thread which does not break.
Stay close by us this day.

Even as we sing praise to the ascending Christ,
we want to cling to the Jesus we know,
for partings leave us confused and bereft.
We do not want to walk alone.

Forgive us that for all our love and devotion,
we remain reluctant to embrace your call
to live in the world
as if we were alone.

Wrap us in the great cloak of your forgiveness
and free us from sufficient doubt that we may be able
to journey with the absent Christ.

229 Great and glorious God, forgive us for the times when our outlook is earth-
bound. So precious is your humanity to us that we forget you are our risen
Lord and our ascended Saviour, and so we fail to proclaim to others that your
Kingdom transcends time and space.

Forgive us our earthbound thoughts. Set us free to lift our eyes to Jesus Christ
reigning in glory, so that we learn to show eternity through the ordinariness
of our every day.

230 Risen, ascending Christ,
you are the song of God leaping through the universe;
you are our lark ascending,
drawing our praises up and beyond this passing day.

You are the sailor back from the sea,
returning to your beginning with earth's human treasure.

You are the warrior home safe from war,
your scars and our pain are now with God.

You are the first-born claiming your heritage,
promising a home for pilgrims who travel the Way.

We celebrate with joy a journey over,
a task accomplished, a promise fulfilled.

To you, our Christ, be glory and gladness for ever.

231 Ascension Lord,
we would have lingered on Transfiguration Mount,
clung to you in the Easter garden,
been saddened by your Emmaus departure,
and begged the Ascension skies never to close.
But you have taught us deeper truth:
you are not absent,
even in departure.

We give thanks
that mountain-top resources lie waiting in the valley,
that you are as near in the busy streets as in the quiet garden,
that you are the guest at every meal,
and heaven has come down to earth,
as one day earth may be as heaven.

Ascension Lord,
travel with us.

Pentecost

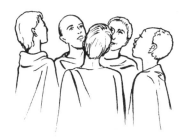

232 Pentecostal God, your presence within the world
we feebly describe as wonder and glory.
We cannot but wonder because although you approach us
in ways volcanic: fire, fear and splendour,
we are neither consumed nor overcome by you.
> Draw near to us this day.
> Come as fire, come as firefly.
> Come as flame and flash in firework splendour.
> Fill the eye, fill the heart, body and soul.
> Fill the sky of our imagination,
> that we may freely give voice to your wonder and glory.

233 Come, Holy Spirit,
come as the robin in the morning,
awakening our hearts
with your song.

Come as the dove at evening,
bringing blessing and peace.

Come as the blackbird at noonday,
gladdening your world with joy.

Come to us
as we come to worship,
that we may
sing to the Creator,
seek healing for the wounds of creation
and find peace
through active prayer.

234 Come, Holy Spirit, blow among us
as we celebrate your calling us out
to be the people of God:
  birthday of the Church.

Come, Holy Spirit, rain upon us
as we celebrate your showering of gifts
on the people of God:
  empowering the Church.

Come, Holy Spirit, shine between us
as we celebrate your awakening us to the vision
of all people on earth
  as the Church of God.

235 How will we speak the name beyond all names?
We will light a flame to proclaim God is among us.

How will we praise the one who knew the cold embers of death for us?
We look into consuming flame and say 'behold the Lamb of God'.

How will we celebrate the Mystery, the Spirit, the Companion among us?
We clap the hands of our hearts,
for she it is who makes each one a home for Christ.

God of fire, we shrink from your justice
but adore the love which fuels it.

Christ, blaze of God's fire spent upon our darkness,
we are stilled and silenced by your passion and death.

Dancing Spirit-flame, you awaken us to the risen Christ,
you invite us to sing and dance in our heart;
and for this we open the most secret places of our being
in adoration and wonder.

236 Fierce Spirit of God, we welcome you!
We know we are dry bones,
and though you must first discomfort us,
we long to flex our muscles:
    to breathe and dance in harmony
    and rediscover community.

Fierce Spirit of God, we invite you to stay!
We know we have restricted areas within us
and though we dread your two-edged sword,
we long to be pierced and opened to you:
    to have hidden disease cut away
    and inner pain healed.

Fierce Spirit of God, we offer you our love!
We know we are slow and blind,
and though you must shake and remake us,
we long to understand:
    to see with Emmaus eyes
    and live the resurrection life.

237 God of flame and colour, your life has flowed through our history, leaping
from one generation to another, releasing captives, affirming the poor, welcoming outcasts. You have spoken with the accent of all people in displaying
your love for all life.

We confess to you and to each other our drabness and uniformity;
Our desire to control rather than share your life;
To reproduce the past rather than explore the future;
We confess the narrowness of our vision,
and our choosing of the most comfortable path.

God of flame and colour, dance around us, enchant us, quicken us and above
all forgive us for painting your gospel in the dowdy colours of our limiting
culture. Release us from the prisons of our own making. In the name of Christ.

238 God who connects us, who relates and reconciles,
forgive us when we fragment your world.
>To our Babels, bring your Pentecost;
>**Teach us the language of understanding and unity.**

Forgive us when we undermine our neighbours
instead of encouraging them.
>To our Babels, bring your Pentecost;
>**Teach us the language of understanding and unity.**

Forgive us when we close ranks in hostility
instead of opening ourselves in hospitality.
>To our Babels, bring your Pentecost;
>**Teach us the language of understanding and unity.**

Forgive us when we pursue self-interest
instead of sharing resources and power.
>To our Babels, bring your Pentecost;
>**Teach us the language of understanding and unity.**

Forgive us when we are diverted by trivia
instead of engaging with the struggles of the downtrodden.
>To our Babels, bring your Pentecost;
>**Teach us the language of understanding and unity.**

Forgive us when we rape the earth
instead of respecting and cherishing it.
>To our Babels, bring your Pentecost;
>**Teach us the language of understanding and unity.**

God who connects us, who relates and reconciles,
forgive us when we fragment your world.

239 God of many voices, time and again you have filled the lives and voices of
your people with your Word, which has been to the world like the leaping,
crackling flames of a bush or forest fire.
At this season of Pentecost, we focus our thankfulness upon the voice and the
vision you gave to a struggling group of believers.
We give thanks for voices and accents, other than our own, which speak to us
of Christ, deepening our experience and widening our vision.

We give thanks for martyr voices like Stephen, among the first disciples, Joan of Arc, and Romero of El Salvador, and all who have not been afraid to speak your Word, and whose directness undermines our clever evasions.

We give thanks that the rich variety within the Christian Church still speaks of the day 'they all heard in their own tongue'.

We give thanks for Christ, who is for us the voice of all ages proclaiming the Word of God within the world.

240 Thank you, kaleidoscope God,
for the strong colours of Pentecost!

Thank you
    for blue and green:
        rippling and raging, scouring and roaring
        in gales of the Spirit, winds of change.

Thank you
    for red and yellow:
        sparking and blazing, leaping and alighting
        in tongue of fire, torches of courage.

Thank you
    for white and silver:
        quieting and consoling, inspiring and soaring
        in dove of peace, messenger of hope.

Thank you for all these colours
    of love and longing,
    of wildness and wisdom,
    challenge and compassion.
So colour our lives by your mighty Spirit,
    that we change,
    find courage,
    radiate hope,
for this is thanksgiving
more precious than words.

241 Today we celebrate! We have found our tongues!
We can whisper our wonder,
     sing aloud our joy,
     speak out about our concerns,
     shout from the rooftops
     our enthusiasm and love
and be heard and understood.

But also we think of people who have no voice.
We grieve for those who are poor, powerless, silenced:
     those so depressed that they feel they have nothing worthwhile to say,
     those tongue-tied or locked in shyness,
     those who are brain damaged, or have speech impediments;
those neither heard nor understood.
     O God, as Jesus came to one afflicted,
     come to such as these
     with your healing word:
          Ephphatha!
          Be opened!

242 *Wind of God,*
blowing from the four corners of the earth,
breathe on us,
our bones are dried up and our hope is lost.
Breathe hope and sinew into our desolate spirits.

In flooded village,
in refugee camp,
in hungry homes,
may your arm be under the head of the helpless,
may they rise up from the graveyard of despair
and find new life through the power of love.

Hurricane of God,
blowing across the universe,
stir the hearts of the compassionate,
overturn the caution of the hesitant,
that the resources of the world
may be shared with the hungry,
that tanks may be turned into tractors,
and the debt of millions cancelled.

Breath of God
gently whispering in our ears,
remove the dust of apathy
which clouds our vision.
Energize us,
that we may be
a source of comfort for the sick,
of solace for the bereaved.
Holy Spirit of comfort and change,
send us out in confidence and joy
to keep the faith and share it.

243 We pray for the universal community of Christians, that we may remain faithful to the diversity God gave the Church at Pentecost.
    Upon every community of believers: **Blow, Spirit, blow.**

For the Church called into being in one era but who finds difficulty adapting to new times.
    Upon every community of believers: **Blow, Spirit, blow.**

For all congregations and communities who honour and serve Christ in and through the poor and the wretched of the earth.
    Upon every community of believers: **Blow, Spirit, blow.**

For the leaders of the nations and their representatives, that they may break through barriers of diplomacy, self-interest and culture and discover the freedom, joy and justice God alone can give.
    Upon every community of believers: **Blow, Spirit, blow.**

Within our cities, towns and villages may God's spirit energize skill and resourcefulness, that the life which flows out of communities may be shared and celebrated as the strength of all.
    Upon every community of believers: **Blow, Spirit, blow.**

For teachers, doctors, nurses, social workers, housing officers, planners and all who carry a direct share in adding to the common good.
    Upon every community of believers: **Blow, Spirit, blow.**

For the overworked and the under-employed; for the overpaid and the desperate poor; for the glamorous and the plain, for the strong and the weak.
    Upon every community of believers: **Blow, Spirit, blow.**

244 When dawn's ribbon of glory around the world returns
and the earth emerges from sleep,
may the shadow of the dove be seen,
as she flies across moor and city.
Over the warm breast of the earth she skims,
her shadow falling on the watcher in the tower,
the refugee in the ditch,
the weary soldier at the gate.

May her shadow of peace
fall across the all-night sitting of a council,
across the tense negotiators around a table.

May her shadow of hope
be cast across the bars of a hostage cell,
filling with momentary light
rooms tense with conflict;
bringing a brief respite,
a slither of gold across the dark.

May she fly untiring across flooded fields,
across a city divided by hate and fear,
across a town wreathed in smoke.

May the shadow of reconciliation;
the dove of peace with healing in her wings,
be felt and seen, and turned towards,
as she makes righteousness shine like the dawn,
the justice of her cause like the noonday sun.

245 God of wind, blow strongly in the world,
bursting through structures of injustice and scattering the dust of apathy;
cooling the heated frenzy of those who know only violent means of
expression or resentment;
stirring into life all who are wearied by failure,
silenced by ridicule,
or too cowed to imagine a better life.

God of fire, burn brightly in the world,
   cauterizing the wounds we have inflicted on the poor by our greed;
   melting the hearts of those who have grown hard and cold,
      who refuse to recognize and name evil;
   giving light to all who identify with the oppressed,
      and work with them to reclaim their dignity.

God of wind and fire, fill this house where we are sitting:
   the house of our own life,
   the house of the church,
   the house of the world.
Where there is division or hurt,
   heal and harmonize us.
Where there is disintegration or a falling apart,
   re-connect and reconcile us.
Where there is rigidity or an over-respectability,
   lighten, loosen, leaven us,
   make us laugh at ourselves
and respond to your free and unpredictable Spirit.

246 God, whose presence was in the burning bush,
   barefoot we stand before you;
God whose power was in rushing wind and tongues of flame,
   amazed we stand before you.
Quietly and deliberately we tighten our grip upon our vocation
as friends and followers of Jesus.

Deepen our resolve,
open our eyes to ways of witnessing,
quicken our hands to ways of service,
renew in us a spirit of prayer,
that we may live the fire of God
with passion and tenderness day by day.

We sense your glory in that you fill us to overflowing
with no sense of waste or worry;
you entrust us
and empower with all that you are.

God of burning bush, rushing wind and tongues of flame,
renew us in your service.

247 Spirit of God, giver of wonderful gifts,
we have so little to offer you or the world.
   Our love is tainted by self-absorption;
   our joy is undermined by lack of trust;
   our peace is disturbed by our fractiousness;
   our patience is bruised by our greedy rush for gain;
   our kindness is weakened by thought of reward;
   our goodness is spoiled by cruel words and thoughtless actions;
   our fidelity is worn away by our fascination with short-term goals;
   our gentleness is wounded by our lack of attention;
   our self-control is warped by careless indiscipline of mind, body and spirit.

What can we give you, who gives all to us?
   We offer our poverty and failure
   lest, in waiting until we are richer and better,
   we offer nothing at all.

248 Give us, ever-patient God, that spirit
   which can endure delay,
   and bear suffering,
   and never give in.
To endure delay,
   yet live through each moment with confidence,
   and not lose heart,
   nor allow the vision of the better times to fade.
To bear suffering,
   yet not be broken by it,
   and not be overcome by bitterness,
   nor find faith fall short.
And never give in,
   yet not to bear a grudge
   and not to live, grim-faced, stiff-lipped,
   nor show pride in enduring.
But rather, by your Spirit, point us to Jesus our Lord who, through temptations, injustice, hardship and opposition patiently bore your perfect will with loving kindness and with constant hope.

Trinity

249 Be with us, God,
Stay with us as we worship,
Loving Father, parent of all who gather here,
Jesus Christ, our brother,
Holy Spirit, spirit of wisdom and love,
> Be with us,
> Stay with us,
> Go with us,
> God, three in one, we worship you.

250 God, Creator, Son and Holy Spirit,
you have unfolded before our eyes
the story of salvation,
amazing to us all.

You are the Source of breath;
you are the Word made flesh;
you are the Spirit of Life.

You are the Maker;
you are the Jesus-Man;
you are Holy Energy.

You are for us;
You are with us;
You are ahead of us.

You are Source, Life, Goal;
yesterday, today, for ever.

You are GOD.

Alleluia!

251 God, three in one and one in three,
>   we seek you in faith
>   and worship you.
Creator, you made us in your image,
Christ, you saved us from our sin,
Spirit, you live and move in us.
All-encompassing, eternal God,
hear our prayer and give us your blessing.

252 No words, living God,
can describe you,
>   define you,
>   capture you.
You are more than all human language;
you are beyond human understanding.

Yet we glimpse you in the majesty of the universe;
we sense you in the wonder of birth;
we feel you in the beauty of nature.

For this, we adore you and praise your name.

Then, in Jesus, you show us your face,
clearer than we ever deserved,
a face which smiles upon us,
eyes which weep with us,
lips which speak forgiveness,
arms which reach out to welcome us.

For this, we adore you and praise your name.

And that is just the beginning.
You never stop disclosing your purpose to us.
By your Spirit you move among us,
producing unity and community,
gifts of faith, hope and love.

For this, we adore you and praise your name.

253 God,
Creator of all that was and is and is to be,
Parent of your children, made in your image,
you gave us life, you give us love,
we praise and adore you.

God,
Jesus, the Son who taught and healed and loved,
Christ, the Redeemer who died and rose and lives for ever,
you guide our lives, you guide us in love,
we praise and adore you.

God,
Holy Spirit, Wisdom who inspires us,
the Comforter who sustains us,
you fill us with faith, you fill us with love,
we praise and adore you.

God, Parent, Son and Spirit,
without you we would not be,
with you we are holy and precious people.
All praise and honour be yours.

254 How do we adore what we do not see?
We love the great God of earth and of sea;
We follow the Saviour who set us all free;
We trust the True One in you and in me;
And do all these things in humility.

Three in one and one in three,
Ever-loving Trinity,
Not a secret mystery,
But seen in one who came to be,
To live, and know, and die for me:
Jesus Christ of Galilee.
Hallelujah! Glory be!
Total Christianity.

255 Timeless God, Creator of the Universe, you alone sustain the space our world inhabits; you alone are worthy of the gladness and praise of our lives.

You exist in ways we cannot imagine and dwell in a splendour we feebly name as your glory. The light of your presence accompanies us and the goodness of your ways surrounds us.

You approach us in humility and weakness, willing to be misunderstood or ignored for the sake of love.

We adore the mystery that combines the unspoken and the uttered, the eternal with the momentary, the universal with the particular, for through such paradox we experience your holiness.

Jesus, for us the Christ, our Brother, our Companion, you are the unmasking of God, flesh of our flesh and bone of our bone.

You laid aside your glory and became a servant, ready and willing to respond to God's call for a new world. You shared our life and in the end succumbed to the powerful in the name of love. To you belongs all the gladness our hearts can muster.

Mysterious spirit, always brooding, always moving; you continue to lead us in the dance disclosed to us in Jesus; your living presence is our strength and peacefulness. You are the search for life that makes us restless; you are the truth of life that allows us to be still.

To you belongs all the welcome and delight of our hearts, for you are the pleasure of Christ among us.

We open ourselves in gladness and commitment to the way of the Cross and the life of your Kingdom.

256 Three-Person God,
you are holy, holy, holy,
yet nothing can separate us from your love.

You are maker of heaven and earth,
yet you know each of us through and through.

You are judge and Lord of all,
yet you are marvellous in mercy.

You are perfect in Christ,
yet you embrace imperfect human beings.

You are the Eternal Word,
yet you speak to each of our hearts.

You are the Light of the universe,
yet you brighten each of our paths.

You are the King of kings and Lord of lords,
yet you die helpless on a cross.

You are the Spirit of Eternal Love,
yet you are experienced in mother, father, child,
                    in friend and neighbour.

You are unchanging and eternal,
yet you create new heavens and a new earth.

You are the Beginning and End,
yet you touch every moment of our lives.

Three-Person God,
we will never cease to praise you.

257 God, Creator of all the universe,
we thank you for all that you have made:
for land and sea, air, fire and light;
    all make the universe what it is,
    designed and ordered by your wisdom.

We search its mysteries, rejoice in its beauty,
revel in its joys, and struggle to understand when it causes suffering.
    But without you we would not exist
    and life would be nothing.

God, divine Son Jesus,
we thank you for all you have done:
    for your saving work on the cross,
    your resurrection and ascension,
    your mediation for our needs,
    your selfless love and obedience.
We study your words, admire your deeds,
follow your example, knowing we can never reach your perfection.
    But without you we would be condemned to death
    and life would be nothing.

God, Holy Spirit,
we thank you for being with us, in us;
    we depend on your guidance,
    rely on your inspiration,
    seek your gifts,
    and try to show your fruits.
        But without you we would be empty
        and life would be nothing.

Give us good things, generous God,
so that we can truly live Christian lives,
and share you with our neighbours.

258 Three-in-one God,
three things we ask of you:
that we may see you more clearly,
    love you more dearly,
    follow you more nearly,
    day by day.

May we see you more clearly
in the world around us,
in the needs of our neighbours,
in the social and political events of history.

May we love you more dearly
in the delight of worship and devotion,
in the challenge of service,
in the enthusiasm with which we tell people about you.

May we follow you more nearly
into the places where people are struggling for justice,
into the wilderness of people's grief and pain,
into the situations where peace is absent.

Three-in-one God,
strengthen and sustain us
as we seek to be your people
day by day.

259 I bind myself to you this day in love, holy God.
I give glory to you, God my Father,
    for you love me and I love you.
I give glory to you, Jesus the Son,
    for, by your love, you have saved me.
I give glory to you, Holy Spirit,
    for your guidance, gifts and grace.

Strengthen me, sustain me, fill me with faith,
that I may worship and serve you all my days.

260 God our Parent, you love us with a generous heart,
we love you and seek to show our love in our giving.
God the Son, you love us enough to give your life for us,
we love you and try to show our love in our living.
God the Spirit, you love us and fill us with blessings,
we love you and wish to show our love in the fruits of our serving.

God, in so many ways you reveal your love for us,
strengthen our faith
so that we may show our love for you in our loving of others.

All Saints

261 Let us worship the Lord
with Christians of every time and place!

Worship the Lord in faith!
For he is our constant and trustworthy God,
the same yesterday, today and forever.

Worship the Lord in hope!
For he is our saving and healing God,
who brings his people from darkness into light.

Worship the Lord in love!
For he is our generous and merciful God,
who blesses and nurtures all his saints.

Let us worship the Lord together
with joy in our hearts.

262 Lord, come to us:
as once you came to Elijah in a cave on a mountain;
as once you came to Isaiah in the temple;
as once you came to travellers on the road in the breaking of bread.

Lord, come to us:
as you come to the woman who cries out because her child has no food;
as you come to the prisoner tortured for standing up for the truth;
as you come to the Aids sufferer shunned by society.

Lord, come to us:
as you came to our mothers and fathers in the faith;
as you came to Columba, Patrick, Boniface, Mother Julian and John Huss;
as you came to those who well served you, though with no place in the
history books.

Lord, come to us, and continue to come;
affirm our faith, comfort our sadness and disturb our complacency.

263 Creator of the universe,
    your handiwork delights us,
    your care for us nurtures us,
    your steadfastness upholds us.
    Creator of the universe,
        With all your saints   **we worship you.**

    Jesus Christ, Son of God,
    your coming as a man astounds us,
    your word of life awakens us,
    your rising from death transforms us.
    Jesus Christ, Son of God,
        With all your saints   **we worship you.**

    Holy Spirit, Breath of Life,
    your vitality empowers us,
    your fire illuminates us,
    your powerful love unites us.
    Holy Spirit, Breath of Life,
        With all your saints   **we worship you.**

264 We never worship you alone, Lord God. Even when we are on our own we
are still surrounded by your faithful people from the past, in the present, and
of the future.
Women and men have been prepared to die to serve you, Lord God.
Your love has had such an amazing effect on them.
Ordinary people, like us, have done extraordinary things, Lord God.
Your spirit has transformed them.
We have been given hope that there is a purpose for life, Lord God.
You have met us in Jesus.
So, with all your people of every age, we come to praise and adore you.

265 Loving God, we thank you
    for all those who have listened to your call,
    followed you faithfully,
    served you wholeheartedly
    and witnessed to your truth, justice and love.

We thank you for the prophets
who bravely declared your word
to hostile and uncaring peoples.
We thank you for the disciples
who embraced the strange adventure
of following Jesus.
We thank you for the evangelists
who risked their lives to bring the good news
of your saving love to all the world.

We thank you for Christian people
in every age and in every place,
who have lived out your gospel
as shining lights in a dark world.
We remember those whom we have known,
who have shown us the way of love
and given us insights, comfort or challenge.
We thank you now for those who have died,
and rejoice that in you we are all made one
on earth and in heaven.

266 For the faithful people whose stories are told in the Bible:
Sarah, Ruth and Priscilla;
Jacob, Hosea and John.
We praise and thank you, Lord.

For the faithful people in the long history of the Church:
Julian, Theresa and Elisabeth;
Columba, Augustine and Martin.
We praise and thank you, Lord.

For faithful people in the news today:
Name those currently in the news.
We praise and thank you, Lord.

For faithful people in this congregation:
Invite the congregation to think of people for whose lives they are grateful.
We praise and thank you, Lord.

Lord we thank you for your love shown in the lives of all your saints:
those who lived in the past and those living now;
those whose names are well known
and those whose names are only known to you.

Part 2
The Parallel Christian Year

Special Sundays

Bible Sunday

267 Our Bibles before us, Lord, we ask you:
open our eyes to read your word,
open our ears to hear your word,
open our hearts to heed your word,
so that our lives may reflect the Living Word, Jesus Christ.

268 For the times when we have rejected your word,
For the times when we have ignored your word,
For the times when we have forgotten your word,
God, the Living Word,
Forgive us.

269 When we read the Bible out of habit rather than with loving eagerness;
For closed book and closed mind: **Forgive us, Lord.**

When we read the Bible without understanding;
For closed book and closed mind: **Forgive us, Lord.**

When we read the Bible seeking comfort without judgement;
For closed book and closed mind: **Forgive us, Lord.**

When we read the Bible seeking joy without discipline;
For closed book and closed mind: **Forgive us, Lord.**

When we read the Bible seeking forgiveness without renewal;
For closed book and closed mind: **Forgive us, Lord.**

Help us so to read that the Spirit may open our minds and lives to your word
for each one of us.

270   Forgive us, Lord, we have limited your voice to a single book.
We have read our newspapers as though you could not speak through them.
We have not listened for you in the skill of the novelist, the imagination of the
poet, the vision of the musician, or the insight of the television producer.
Caging you in a black-bound book, we have silenced you.
Forgive us, Lord.
Speak where you will
and give us ears to hear.

271   Living God,
   free as the air and more boundless than oceans,
   held by no chain and hindered by no restriction;
   God before any beginning and reaching beyond all ends,
   how could we do it?
      We build a church and imprison you within it,
         as though its walls could keep you in.
      We write a creed and hold you to it,
         as though the human mind could well define you.
      We speak of you with such finality,
         as though human thought could express you fully.
      We buy a book and bind it fast,
         as though the written page could describe you.
   We confess our folly.

   Living God,
      leap the walls of the church,
      break the stranglehold of human words and thought,
      escape the pages of every book
      and be yourself
      in your own world.

272   For all who trusted God:
      men and women who dreamed dreams,
      poets who expressed the reality of human life,
      historians who recorded the growth of a nation,
      prophets who challenged the people with the word of God,
      for all the words of the Old Testament,
         we give thanks.

For all who trusted God:
>   men and women who dreamed dreams,
>   disciples who responded to the call of Christ,
>   Jesus, who lived and loved, died and rose again,
>   for those who kept a record of God's action amongst them,
>   for letter-writers who challenged and reassured the young Church,
>   for all the words of the New Testament,
>   we give thanks.

273 With thanksgiving this day, O God, we remember all those who lived and worked, and even died, that we might have the Bible in our own tongue. We remember the scholars of today who spend their lives studying languages, translating the Scriptures and publishing Bibles so that everyone, everywhere, might read of your love.

274 Leading God,
>   you called Abraham out from his native land and sent him on a pilgrimage.
> Liberating God,
>   you broke the tyrant's yoke and called Moses to deliver your people.
> God of community,
>   you gave your people a new land and called David to create a nation.
> Prophetic God,
>   you spoke to Amos in the market-place, calling his generation to justice;
>   to Isaiah in the royal court, calling Israel to face the future;
>   to Hosea at home, declaring your forgiving love.
> Supporting God,
>   you comforted your people in exile and gave vision to Ezra and Nehemiah.
> Suffering God,
>   you stood alongside Jesus in Gethsemane loss and Calvary desolation.
> Boundless God,
>   you opened Paul's eyes and caused the infant Church to break barriers of race.
> Travelling God,
>   you have ever walked with your Church to take us into your future.
> God of every age and time,
>   for the Bible which offers us the story of your presence in every generation,
>   we give you grateful thanks.

275 Lord, we pray:
For scholars and workers involved in Bible translation,
    that they may be given patience and sensitivity
    as they learn new languages, develop skills and increase their vocabulary.
For technicians and printers involved in Bible publication,
    that they may be always aware of the importance of their task,
    offering Bibles that people can afford and in a language they understand.
For all who distribute Bibles through shops and personal contact,
    that their attitude and zeal may commend the book they sell.
For ministers, pastors and teachers who seek to bring the Bible to life,
    that in preaching and teaching they may faithfully interpret its message.
Through Christ the living Word of God.

276 Lord God of every generation,
Remembering how scribes patiently copied the words of the Bible,
    we commit ourselves patiently to study the life-giving word.
Remembering how psalmists joyfully offered their songs to the temple worship,
    we commit ourselves to offer you our praise.
Remembering how gospel-writers faithfully recorded their experience,
    we commit ourselves to share the good news with others.
Remembering Paul's encouragement and challenge to the young churches,
    we commit ourselves to the life of our church.
Remembering how John accepted exile for the sake of the gospel,
    we commit ourselves to the proclamation of the Kingdom.

But this we ask Lord,
in study and song, in evangelism and church life,
and in persecution if such should come,
then as you walked with those we now remember,
walk also with us.

New Year

277 God of all ages, God before beginning
and without end;
you who exist and move among the planets,
draw close to us this day.

God beyond time, you alone come to us
from the future and the past,
filling the present with the flow
of your renewing life.

At the turning of the year, approach us again
that we may draw upon your strength
and drink fully of your tenderness
and know your presence within our journey.

At this beginning time, begin again with us.

278 How can we do anything else but praise you, eternal God?
The year has turned again and brought us to its new beginning;
    the whole earth and the universe beyond shout aloud your glory;
    stars dance with delight at your creative power;
    rivers and streams flow with jubilant strength;
    moonlight and sunlight beam their pleasure;
    whilst the hills around us stand in silent testimony to your greatness.
    All tell of your new-creating power,
    and we join in their praise.

How can we do anything else but praise you?
The year is freshly dawned;
    men and women unite to rejoice in you,
    girls and boys clap their hands at the sound of your name,
    young people cheer your mighty acts,
    all nations, races, colours and ages add their timeless voices,
    and we join in their praise.

Eternal God,
How can we do anything else but praise you?
The depth of winter shines with light!
    You sent Jesus Christ to be light in a dark world;
        he is truth to our ignorance,
        a way for our faltering feet,
        life and health in the sickness of our sin and folly.
    You gave the gift of the Spirit to encourage and guide us.
    You called us into the community of the Church,
        where those who love you worship you
        in each succeeding year,
        and we join in their praise.

How can we do anything else but praise you?
Forgive us that the way we live does not always match the way we worship.
Forgive us for our lack of friendship to each other.
Forgive us our neglect of your creation,
and by your love's tremendous glory,
new-born from year to year,
renew us, and make us whole.

279 God of mercy, renew our life
with your forgiveness,
that, with Christ, we may rise above
what lies behind us
and discover that which your love
has prepared for us.

With sincere hearts we look to you,
for we know only too well how often we have failed;
how often we have wilfully or foolishly abandoned
our resolve to walk the Way of the Cross.
We know we are sinners and admit it to each other
and to you.

As time has taken for ever the old year from us,
so by your grace remove from us all
the death and folly of our sin;
that, being restored by you, we may continue our pilgrimage
as friends and followers of Jesus.

280 Almighty God, you set the spinning planets in their places,
creating the beauty of the earth and the heavens.
You ensured night would follow day, that we might measure our days
and learn to inhabit our years,
and for that we give you thanks.

Into our world of spinning wonder you came
in a way we could recognize, in human form.
For the life of Jesus,
whose birth lit the heavens with new light,
we give you thanks.

Within our world of deceit and betrayal,
you committed your own life for our good,
sharing our pain and regenerating our joy.
For the enduring wonder of the work of Christ
we give you thanks on this and every day.

281 Persisting God:
the passing years do not dim your memory,
nor stop your ears, nor dim your eyes.

In your mercy,
call to mind the prayers we offered
in the year that has passed.
We offer you again the pain, the pity, the horror,
the grief and the daily necessity
which filled our hearts and minds.

Draw together the gathering of prayers
which we have offered throughout the year,
and tenderly bless, dear Lord.

We pray this day for those who find excitement
and renewal in seasons of change;
– whisper in their hearts the things which endure.
We pray also for those who find beginnings and endings hard;
– assure them of your continuing companionship.

In the darkness which is ahead, be our guide;
In the pain which awaits us, be our balm;
In the sorrow which will fill us, be our secret smile;
In the sickness which will inflict us, be our inner health;
In the laughter which will be part of us, be our lasting joy.

We offer you this bundle of prayers
as we begin this year.
Draw them close together in your hands
and hold them to your heart,
and tenderly bless, dear Lord.

282 Journeying God,
you have woven the pattern of your purpose
in and out of the fabric of our years
with a precision and tenderness
we have hardly noticed.

As we look back over the years of our life,
we can see the movement of your hand;
the fruits of your love;
the gentle unfolding of your purpose.

Grant us this day your grace,
that we may not snatch at your purpose for us,
but rather yield to the rhythm and flow
of your love in our lives.

We pray that the days and the nights,
the weeks and the months which are to come
may truly belong to you
for we choose to journey with you.

283 I make my circuit
in the fellowship of God:
on the moor and through the meadow;
on the cold, heathery hill;
on the corner in the open;
on the chill, windy dock;
to the noise of drills blasting;
to the sound of children asking.

I make my circuit
in the fellowship of God:
    in city street;
    or on spring-turfed hill;
    in shop-floor room;
    or at office desk.

God has no favourite places.
There are no special things.
All are God's and all are sacred.

I tread each day
in light or dark
in the fellowship of God.

Be the sacred Three of Glory
interwoven with our lives
until the One who walks it with us
leads us home
through death to life.

(Based on a prayer from the Carmina Gadelica)

284 Lord Jesus Christ,
you were a whole person;
complete and fulfilled.
Your word was your action,
and your actions matched your words.
    At the turning of the year,
    we commit ourselves to marry word and deed,
    and thus to follow you.

Lord Jesus Christ,
Man of God you were,
and man of the people.
    At the turning of the year,
    we commit ourselves to serve the living God
    and care for all his people,
    and thus to follow you.

Week of Prayer for Christian Unity

285
Sisters and brothers, let us weave together!
Let us make a beautiful carpet for the Household of God!
Let us bring the treasures of our various traditions,
the different colours of our insights,
the many-textured threads of our lives in community,
and our rich stories of God's moving in our midst –
and let us weave these strands together
on the Spirit's loom!

Sisters and brothers, let us dance together!
Let us make a graceful circle in the Household of God!
Let us bring our singing and chanting,
the intricate steps of sermon and of silence,
the reaching up of prayer and meditation,
and the choreography of the mission of God –
and let us move together in the dance
to the Spirit's music!

286
We worship you, the one God.
God and Father of our Lord Jesus Christ.
God of Catholic and Protestant, Orthodox and Pentecostal.
God of individual relationship and common faith.
God worshipped in every language and in each land.
God worshipped in ornate ritual and in quiet simplicity.
God worshipped in soaring cathedral and in mud-brick hut.
The same God;
Their God and our God;
Always, everywhere, one God.

287

' ... the Church is meant to be ... a laboratory of peace, a parable of the Kingdom,
a sign of contradiction among the nations,
a place of welcome amidst the sectarianism and xenophobia of the surrounding society,
a community of praise.'

(From *Belonging* by Brother Leonard of Taizé)

Go-between-God, bridge-builder, community-maker:

You call us, your Church,
    to be a laboratory of peace:
accept our sorrow for the hostilities we harbour
and the walls we continue to build.

You call us, your Church,
    to be a parable of the Kingdom:
accept our sorrow for telling a very different story:
a story of attachment to worldly values.

You call us, your Church,
    to be a sign of contradiction:
accept our sorrow for being content with the way things are
and fearful of speaking the prophetic word.

You call us, your Church,
    to be a place of welcome and warmth:
accept our sorrow for sour faces, cold hands,
judgemental attitudes and lack of compassion.

You call us, your Church,
    to be a community of praise:
accept our sorrow for allowing anxiety about human failures
to muzzle confidence in your power to transform the world.

288 A Meditation

My neighbours speak with a different accent and live a different lifestyle.
They choose different plants for their garden and put different curtains in the
windows. Because they are different, I build a wall. Maybe not a wall of bricks
or fence panels but a barrier nevertheless. I'm not rude to them but I don't get
to know them either. It's not worth it, they're different. We wouldn't have
anything in common.

People at that other church talk in a different way about faith and organize church life differently too. Their building is different and their worship is different. Because they are different, I build a wall. Not a wall of hatred or persecution but a barrier nevertheless. I'm not rude to them but I don't get to know them either. It's not worth it, they're different. We wouldn't have anything in common.

Let us pray in silence for God's forgiveness for the barriers we build.

Hear the good news:
So he came and proclaimed the good news: peace to you who were far off, and peace to those who were near; for through him we both alike have access to the Father in the one Spirit.

(Ephesians 2.17-18)

289 *This prayer of thanksgiving uses the simple act of lighting night-lights or candles. The first one should be taller than the others, and central. Each sentence is offered by a different voice, and the prayer works best if people are gathered in a circle.*

I light a candle for Jesus, the Christ.
> **Thanks be to God.**

I light a candle for the apostles, sent out to be Christ's Church.
> **Thanks be to God.**

I light a candle for the Scriptures, Hebrew and Christian, in which we may discern the word that enlivens us.
> **Thanks be to God.**

I light a candle for the wise thinkers – the Fathers and Mothers – of the early Church.
> **Thanks be to God.**

I light a candle for theologians through the ages: for their learning and study and new insights.
> **Thanks be to God.**

I light a candle for the faithful people of God, in whose love and lives the ongoing Church of Christ is realized.
> **Thanks be to God.**

I light a candle for worship – colourful and quiet, exuberant and contemplative: for word and silence, movement and stillness, singing and sighing.
> **Thanks be to God.**

I light a candle for Christian art and literature and music, and for symbols which point us to God.
> **Thanks be to God.**

I light a candle for strength of conviction.
> **Thanks be to God.**

I light a candle for questioning, for journeying in the wilderness, and living on the edge.
> **Thanks be to God.**

I light a candle for our rich diversity.
> **Thanks be to God.**

I light a candle for our blessed connectedness in the love of Christ.
> **Thanks be to God.**

290

Beckoning Christ,
you call us out of our comfortable ghettos
of 'us' and 'them'
to risk discipleship without walls.

> You call us into a world-wide fellowship
> where God is worshipped
> above all other.

> You call us into a world-wide fellowship
> where prayer is offered
> day and night.

> You call us into a world-wide fellowship
> where we can share what we are
> with others who love you.

> You call us into a world-wide fellowship
> where each person has something to give
> to the whole.

> You call us into a world-wide fellowship
> where compassion and respect
> shape missionary endeavour.

Keep on beckoning us
out of our safe havens
into your richer fellowship
of challenge and reconciliation, faith and hope.

291   Eternal God, you have made us one people, your Christian family on earth.
As Christians pray together,
   help us to grow in our relationship with you and each other.
As Christians worship together,
   give us a vision of what your love can do beyond our wildest dreams.
As Christians share the good news together,
   make our unity a witness to the reconciling power of your love.
As Christians feed the hungry together,
   free the Church's resources from selfish use, to meet human need.
As Christians care for the suffering together,
   may the gentle touch which unites our action bring healing to broken lives.
As Christians work for justice and peace together,
   help us to find strength through our faith to resist evil.

Help us to do your will and to receive your gift of unity so that your Kingdom
may come in our lives and in the life of the world.

292   Your people, Lord, are one people.
Your people, Lord, are a holy people.
Your people, Lord, are found in all times and all places.
Your people, Lord, are to work with you for the Kingdom.
We want to be your people, Lord.

293   God of community, three in one,
   we offer ourselves:
      as different organs in a single body;
      as many threads in a woven fabric;
      as diverse stones in a mosaic;
      as various instruments in an orchestra;
      as myriad drops in a moving river.

We acknowledge our need of one another,
our impoverishment when we act alone;
let us find delight in our interdependence
and discover your presence in one another.

Education Sunday

294

Eternal, all-knowing God,
before we call to you,
you have called to us.

Before we have come to know you,
you have loving knowledge of us.
This knowledge is wonderful to us;
it fills us with confidence and delight.

As we worship you this day,
sow in our hearts
the seeds of true knowledge,
the wisdom which makes the world's knowledge seem foolishness,
the awareness that you are our God
and have always been our God.

Enable us to discern your Word
amid all the words we speak,
and all the words we hear;

    to hear your Word
    in the events of our time,
    even though they may be filled with pain and uncertainty;

    to be challenged by your Word
    hidden in the Scriptures we read,
    spoken to our lives,
    to our world,
    and to our churches.

Show us, we pray,
where true wisdom can be found
and where is the place of understanding.

295 Eternal God,
  you call us by your voice,
  as once you made us by your word.
  We are clay in your hands,
    ready to be moulded.
  We are a canvas,
    ready to be painted.
  We are raw material,
    ready to be fashioned.
  Be potter, artist and creator in our lives.

  Open our being to the influence of your spirit,
  so that ears and eyes, heart and mind
  may be alert to your presence;
    ready to learn,
    open to change
    and responsive to truth,
  through Jesus Christ our Lord.

296 All praise to you, eternal Father!
  You are the source of all light and truth.
  You long for your children's growth,
  and your creative power sustains and holds us.

  All praise to you, Lord Jesus Christ!
  You are the Father's gift to us.
  You long to raise us to our true stature,
  and your teaching is our guide, your words our hope.

  All praise to you Holy Spirit of God!
  You are the life of God within us.
  You take the things of Christ and show them to us,
  and you encourage us in our search for truth.

  Father, Son and Holy Spirit:
    Origin of all truth,
    Goal of all learning,
    Beginning and end of all wisdom,
  All praise to you.

297 Gracious God,
we come in a spirit of sadness.
We say we know so much,
but we don't really.

We can glimpse the most distant star,
but we can't see you any clearer.

We can crowd the airwaves with words,
but we can't hear you speaking to us.

We can enable people to see the world from space,
but we can't create global unity.

We can design magnificent buildings,
but we cannot build peace and justice in the community.

We can harness huge resources of power and energy,
but we fail to share the earth's resources.

We can grow mountains of food,
but millions still starve.

We can speak all the languages of the earth,
but we haven't discovered the priority of love.

Forgive us, merciful God.

Show us where true wisdom can be found
and where is the place of understanding.

298 Gracious God,
thank you for all those people down the centuries
who have responded to your presence
and who have communicated this knowledge
to the world with conviction and courage.

For the prophets,
who, knowing you as a God of justice and compassion,
challenged the foolishness of kings and governments
and urged them to walk in wise and responsible paths.

For the song writers,
who, in tumult and sadness, exile and despondency,
wrote new songs for new days
and called on the people to sing of your deeds.

For the wisdom writers,
who, in proverb and parable,
drew the eyes of readers towards goodness,
struggling with the meaning of events,
    the presence of evil
    and the problem of suffering in the world.

For Jesus,
who painted pictures with words,
explained the Kingdom in parables,
and taught his friends the secrets of your way;
Jesus, whose deeds matched his words,
who becomes for us the Way, the Truth and the Life.

For Christian friends we have known,
who, often in hidden and humble ways,
have shown us where wisdom is to be found,
and where is the place of understanding.

299 God of wisdom, on this day, and knowing it to be your purpose that all your
children should grow in understanding and truth, we pray for all those
involved in education:
    for all teachers and lecturers whose work shapes the lives of others;
    for all chaplains in schools, colleges and universities who offer pastoral
        care and seek to interpret the purpose of education in daily life;
    for children and students, that learning may be a joy, and gaining
        knowledge a source of happiness;
    for administrators, that care and efficiency may go hand in hand;
    for all involved in the whole task of education,
        that it may be devoted to justice rather than self-seeking,
        equality rather than privilege,
        and the creation of community rather than division.
We ask this in the name of him who as the Way directs our path, as the Truth
is our purpose and goal, and as the Life is the very spirit by which we live.

300 Welcoming God,
we commend to your care this day
all who tend and nurture young life:
teachers in nursery and primary schools,
parents, grandparents and foster-parents,
sisters and brothers,
all who give energy and commitment
to moulding and shaping children's understanding.

We commend to your care this day
all schools, colleges and universities,
their academic and administrative staff,
students in higher education,
especially those struggling with depression and debt.

We commend to your care this day
those who are involved in religious education;
advising, teaching, or leading worship,
especially where there is apathy and opposition.

We commend to your care this day
scientists and scholars
who uncover knowledge
which can heal or destroy human life.
We remember especially those
who face difficult ethical decisions in their work.

We commend to your care this day
those who, with their knowledge and expertise,
advise governments and leaders
concerning the sharing of resources,
the handling of priorities,
the shape of social provision,
the care of the disadvantaged,
the way medical care is exercised
and the strategies for war and peace.

301 Wise and understanding God,
help us to be eager in the search for wisdom
at all stages in our life.

May we be wise
in our relationships;
faithful to those we love,
tender to those who are bruised,
strong to those who need support.

May we be wise
in our faith;
using our minds to question and explore,
testing our beliefs against our experience,
open and receptive to all who are searching.

May we be wise
in our decision making;
weighing up the implications of our actions,
thinking about their effects on others,
especially those who are disadvantaged.

May we be wise
in our speech;
not only in choosing the words we say
but in taking care over the way we say them,
so that we do not cause needless pain,
but treasure words as precious gifts to share.

May we be wise
in our emotional responses;
trying to balance heart and mind,
taking care when we are angry,
watching when we are under stress.

So may we grow
in wisdom and favour
before you
and one another,
for Jesus' sake.

Christian Aid Week

302 God, our father and our mother,
we, your children, come before you.
We are people with many needs:
    we need food, water, shelter;
    we need the love and companionship of family and friends;
    we need a sense of self-worth and purpose.
And most of all, loving Provider, we need you.
We need you to fill our lives
    with faith and hope and love;
    with comfort and peace and joy.
Giver of every good gift,
you supply our every need.
Accept this, our thank-offering
of worship and praise.

303 All-seeing God, we shut our eyes
to the terrible images of human suffering:
    the mangled bodies of the victims of warfare;
    the swollen bellies and stick-like limbs of the unfed;
    the haunted stare of the beaten and tortured.
       All-seeing God, we confess our self-willed blindness.
       Open our eyes to the suffering of others
       and guide us in our caring.

All-hearing God, we shut our ears
to the heart-rending cries of suffering humanity:
    the shocked mumbling of an orphan child unable to cry;
    the whimpering of a baby held to an empty breast;
    the wailing of the bereaved around an open grave.
       All-hearing God, we confess our self-willed deafness.
       Open our ears to the suffering of others
       and call us to action.

All-knowing God, we shut our minds
to the questions raised by human suffering:
    to the complicated issues of aid and intervention;
    to the painful reality of the depths of human sin;
    to the challenge to our own way of living.
        All-knowing God, we confess our self-willed ignorance.
        Open our minds to the suffering of others
        and enlighten our giving.

304 Creator God,
we thank you for your many gifts to us:
    for the world in all its beauty;
    for food and drink, homes and clothes;
    for people who love us and care for us.
        Help us truly to enjoy your gifts: **Help us to share them with others.**

Saving God,
we thank you for your many gifts to us:
    for your unfailing, forgiving love;
    for the Bread of Life and the True Vine;
    for the Good News for all people.
        Help us truly to enjoy your gifts: **Help us to share them with others.**

Sustaining God,
we thank you for your many gifts to us:
    for the peace and joy that fill our hearts;
    for the impulse to love and serve and give;
    for the love that binds your children together.
        Help us truly to enjoy your gifts: **Help us to share them with others.**

For the sake of Jesus Christ,
who gave all for the humanity he loved,
our Saviour and our Lord.

305 We heard the cry of pain from the baby newly born,
    its mother's breast no comfort.
We saw the child's despair as she trod the lonely road, family separated.
We heard the sad despair of the father out of work, victim of economic policy.
And, Lord, we prayed, collected, gave and loved,
    and though still sad, were glad.

306 Let us pray for all victims of injustice and warfare.
Lord Jesus, you knew the pain of betrayal and the agony of torture.
We remember before you the suffering people of ...
We pray that you might strengthen them,
and that the peoples of the world and their leaders might work
together for justice and peace.
Lord, in your mercy: **Hear our prayer.**

Let us pray for the destitute, the hungry and the homeless.
Lord Jesus, you understood what it was to be poor, hungry, without shelter.
We remember before you those struggling to find the means for life,
the malnourished, the refugees. We remember the people of ...
We pray that they might gain what they need to live
and that the peoples of the world and their leaders might work together
for a fairer sharing of the earth's resources.
Lord, in your mercy: **Hear our prayer.**

Let us pray for all those who work to help the suffering.
Lord Jesus, you fed the hungry, healed the sick, restored sight to the blind.
We remember before you those who work for Christian Aid.
We pray that you will be with them, upholding them and guiding them,
as they work for the coming of your Kingdom of justice and plenty.
Lord, in your mercy: **Hear our prayer.**

307 *'Truly I tell you: anything you did for one of my brothers here, however
insignificant, you did for me.'*

Lord, you are hungry:
we will feed you.

Lord, you are thirsty:
we will give you drink.

Lord, you are a stranger:
we will make you welcome.

Lord, you are naked:
we will clothe you.

Lord, you are in prison:
we will befriend you.

For we, Lord, are the people of your Kingdom,
and we will love and serve you in the world.

Harvest

308 Lord of the harvest,
we offer you our worship.
We adore you and thank you
for the beauty and the bounty
of the world which you have made.
Lord of the harvest,
accept our offering of praise.

309 From the ear the seed,
from the seed the shoot,
from the shoot the stem,
from the stem the leaves,
from the leaves the flower,
from the flower the seed.
Lord of every season,
from seed-time to harvest,
from us to you,
we give our offering of praise and thanksgiving.

310 We praise you, O God, for the gifts of the harvest.
You are the creator of the world!
Everything we see causes us to praise you.

We praise you for our food:
the crunch of an apple and the juice of an orange;
the taste of meat and varieties of fish;
the goodness of vegetables and the luxury of fruit;
the sweetness of sugar and the sharpness of salt;
for milk and tea, and fresh water to quench our thirst.

We praise you for the harvest of industry:
> the products of factory and mill;
> for clothes and cars, for tables and televisions;
> for iron and steel, plastic and petrol
> and for the skill to fashion the materials you created on earth.

This harvest day,
> reminds us afresh that you love us and care for us.
> Call us again to share your task of caring for this world.
> Whisper anew that you created us in your image.

Then we will unite to praise you for the harvest,
to join you in partnership
and offer you these gifts as a thanksgiving
for everything you give us the whole year through.

311 We take an apple from a tree and eat it,
> forgetting your gift of creation.

We pour milk from a jug and drink it,
> forgetting your gift of creation

We buy a packet of food and enjoy it,
> forgetting all that has been done to produce it.

We open a bottle to quench our thirst,
> forgetting all that has been done to produce it.

We throw excess food away from our plates,
> forgetting those who need it.

We let water run down the drain,
> forgetting those who need it.

We pause when faced with abundant variety,
> forgetting those who have no choice at all.

We decide which is our favourite food today,
> forgetting those who have no choice at all.

Loving God, in our plenty we do not appreciate all that we have. Grateful for our abundance, help us not to forget those whose harvest is meagre and limited. Celebrating the harvest, help us not to forget those who bring it to our tables. Genuine in our thanks, help us to be generous in our giving.

312 Lord God, we thank you for our festival day.
We celebrate with thanksgiving your gift of Harvest.

We thank you that we live in a country of abundance.
We enjoy our food and never really go hungry,
Even in drought, the water still flows,
The roof stands firm above our heads.
Offering our gifts today, we pray for those in need of food, drink and shelter.

We pray for the work of ... who will receive our gifts. We thank you for their work in ... We thank you for all who, moved by your love, work to share the gift of life and the joy of living with those whose lives lack the riches we possess. May the help that is given and received be a sign both of our love for them and our love for you. We pray in the name of Jesus who gave all that he had for us.

313 Thanks be to you, our God, for the giving of the harvest.
Thanks for the variety of food,
    which gives enjoyment to our eating.
Thanks for the colours of fruit,
    which give beauty to our table.
Thanks for the diversity of vegetables,
    which gives so much choice.
Thanks for the produce of this country,
    which gives fresh food each day.
Thanks for the produce from overseas,
    which gives ample supplies throughout the year.

Thanks be to you, our God, for the giving of the harvest.
Thanks for all who sow and nurture and reap
    and give us food for growth.
Thanks for all who transport and sell
    and give us the freedom to choose.
Thanks for all who cultivate and improve
    and give us better yields, finer crops.
Thanks for all who prepare and cook
    and give us tasty meals which entice us to eat.
Thanks for all who advise and instruct
    and give us good food for health.

Thanks be to you, our God, for the giving of the harvest.

314 All power and glory are yours: **For ever and ever. Amen.**

We pray, O Father, for those who work to provide our food:
  for the farmer and gardener, the lorry-driver and shopkeeper,
  for the skills you have given to them,
  and the expertise we can use to grow our food.
All power and glory are yours: **For ever and ever. Amen.**

We pray, O Father, for those who have no food:
  for the hungry of the world,
  and for those who, for lack of water or good soil,
    cannot grow enough to live on.
We pray for those who use their power to help others in need,
  for the aid agencies,
  and each individual who gives to help another person.
All power and glory are yours: **For ever and ever. Amen.**

We pray, O Father, for the leaders of the world:
  that they will use their power for the good of all;
  that they will be just and even-handed in making decisions.
We pray for ourselves that, as people rich in comparison with many, we may
learn to reject selfishness, and live in love, as your Son showed us.
All power and glory are yours: **For ever and ever. Amen.**

315 Once more we have celebrated the harvest,
  brought our gifts, sung our hymns and remembered the Creator.
  Lord of the Harvest,
  give us one more gift.
  Help us to remember this festival throughout the coming year
  of ploughing, sowing, feeding, reaping.

  Every time we eat a meal, remind us of your presence.
  Every time we drink, remind us of your blessings.
  Every time we see a need, give us the sense of sharing.
  Every time we enjoy your creation, fill us with thanks and praise,
  so that when we gather again next harvest-time
  we shall know that you have sustained us,
  and we have lived and given ourselves for you.

One World Week

316   All-embracing God, you love everyone as your children.
Here we are: different people from different homes and different backgrounds
but united in faith. Join us with our brothers and sisters around the world in
worship to the glory of your name.

317   Come, let our hearts be glad
and our spirits rejoice,
for God shows us the path of life
and leads us in the ways of peace.
May the seeds of hopefulness
be planted in our hearts today,
and the fruits of hopefulness
blossom and grow within this community.

318   There is neither Jew nor Gentile, slave nor free, man nor woman, just people
who all belong to Christ. Each one is known and named by our heavenly
Father.

God, our Father,
we know that we do not treat people equally.
We are prejudiced towards those who are like us,
and against those who are different from us.
Forgive us for our small-mindedness.
Open our hearts and minds to respect and learn from everyone:
black or white, rich or poor, young or old, woman or man,
for each person is your creation,
each one is brother or sister to the other.
In the name of Jesus, your Son,
who loved without regard to status, wealth or race,
and longs to renew us with his open, understanding love.

319 Who is my neighbour?
Forgive us for despising our neighbours:
the noisy family down the street whose children enjoy loud music,
the family next door whose cooking smells upset our sense of taste,
the family on Social Security whose style of living is not like ours.

Forgive us for despising our neighbours:
the people whose countries we visit on holiday, and make jokes at their
    expense,
the people whose countries produce food for which we pay so little,
the people whose countries we judge from ignorance.

Forgive us for despising our neighbours.
Forgive us for our blinkered attitudes,
    our fettered charity,
    our restrained loving,
    our bitter prejudice
    and our total apathy.

Who is my neighbour?
Each and every child of God!
Thanks be to God.

320 God of all hopefulness:
If we have made gold our hope,
forgive us.
If we have made success our confidence,
forgive us.
If we have rejected the cause of the poor,
forgive us.
If we have rejoiced in the ruin of others,
forgive us,
for in you alone is our hope.
    As you nourished us with hope at the breast,
    as you implanted hope in us as we grew,
    help us to nourish its growth
    in us and in our world.

321
Hope growing,
silently, secretly,
like a child in the womb, fluttering;
putting out soft tentacles,
hope stretching, stirring.

Hope growing,
silently, secretly,
daring to breathe again
as footsteps recede
and danger retreats,
hope stretching, stirring.

Hope growing,
silently, secretly,
swelling, burgeoning, bursting
until the flower opens,
the child is crowned,
the prisoner is released,
and hope is born.

God of all hopefulness:
for seeds of silent growth
and secret expectation
we thank you.
Bring hope to birth in us;
release us that we may worship
in freedom and joy.

322
We thank you, great God, for the wonderful world in which we live:
    full of variety, so that each day is full of new experiences;
    full of excitement, so that each day is never dull;
    full of love, so that each day we are comforted in sorrow and uplifted in joy.

We thank you, great God, for the amazing world in which we live:
    never ceasing to thrill us with its undiscovered beauty;
    never lacking a sense of opportunity;
    never two moments the same.

We rejoice in your world and your people,
    in all that is familiar to us, and all that is new,
    in exploration, sharing, and in enjoying what it means to be one of your
        friends.
Through Jesus Christ, who revealed your creative love.

323 Hope as delicate as a spider's web,
strong as a hawser;
hope lively and lovely:
this is what has been
planted in us and our world,
sometimes nurtured,
grown,
come to flower;
sometimes smashed,
broken,
withered.

Help us,
Creator of Hope,
to recognize its growth,
to secure its planting,
to celebrate its flowering
within our hearts
and throughout your world.

324 If I ignore my brother, I lose,
If I despise my sister, I lose,
If I am withdrawn, I lose,
If I am arrogant, I lose,
If I think only of myself, I lose,
If I trust only in myself, I lose.
But if I am open to what others have to share with me,
ready to receive, and open to give,
eager to love and able to cherish,
I win,
not only for myself but for the whole world.
Help me, O God, so that the needs of the world, and my own needs
are fulfilled by your love.

325 A meditation

Hope is a dark, elusive child
curled in the womb,
cradled in our arms.
It can be lost,
disappear,
blown on the wind like a dandelion clock.

Its going,
its ebbing away
leaves us
grieving,
empty,
hopeless.

'But' is a hopeful word.

But,
even as the gossamer
powder-puff
disintegrates,
the seeds are carried
to cling to distant crevices.
As it recedes
it re-seeds,
to grow again.

God, giver of peace,
grow hope within and around us.
God of steadfast love,
never leave us hopeless.

326

We pray for the world,
torn apart by hatred, rent in two by conflict,
broken by dishonesty, disfigured by cruelty,
full of suspicion, intolerance and loathing.
    Teach us how truly to love,   **that the world may be one.**

We pray for the world,
starving because of selfishness, thirsty for clean water,
cold for want of a roof, dying for lack of medicine,
full of complacency, greed and ignorance.
　　Teach us how truly to love,　　**that the world may be one.**

We pray for the world,
wanting to help and not hinder, willing to give and not receive,
open to share and not to withhold, loving as well as is known,
full of goodwill, ideals and sympathy.
　　Teach us how truly to love,　　**that the world may be one.**

God, who loves fully, truly, deeply,
help us to show our love by actions and words,
so that the world may be united as one,
and all may live in harmony with equality.
In the name of Jesus, who gave himself in love for all.

327　Let us choose hope:
　　jumping ditches,
　　climbing fences,
　　choosing hope;
planning meetings,
preparing dialogue,
choosing hope;
　　digging wells,
　　remaking roads,
　　choosing hope;
getting up,
taking nourishment,
choosing hope.

Lord, in this world
of ethnic cleansing and peace talks,
development and daily living,
when optimism flags,
help us to choose to hope,
and help our hope to grow.

Justice and Peace
General Prayers

328 *Come see what the Lord has done, the astounding deeds he has wrought on earth: he puts an end to war, he breaks the bow, he snaps the spear, he burns the shields in the fire.*

'Be still, and know that I am God.'

God of our ancestors, be with us now.
Still the turmoil in our hearts,
disarm us of the bitterness and resentment with which we wound each other,
help us lower the defences which isolate us from others.
Help us be still.
Help us learn of your love.
Help us worship.
Through Jesus Christ.

329 *Steadfast love and faithfulness will meet; justice and peace will kiss each other.*

Father, as we worship,
make us aware of your love in all generations;
help us respond with faith and praise.

Father, as we worship,
make us aware of your faith in us.
As partners in your work in the world,
help us respond with vision and action,
looking to the time when peace will be possible
because of those who work for justice,
through your Spirit in us, active in the world.

330 Gracious God,
you are Lord of this fine day and of every day.
We gather to give you praise.

Loving God,
you are the source of love,
and out of your compassion
you love even us.
We gather to give you praise.

Eternal God,
you are the source of peace,
bringing concord to conflict,
hope to despair
and comfort to sorrow.
We gather to give you praise.

Liberating God,
you promise freedom:
releasing us from all
that stops us being
true followers of Christ.
We gather to give you praise,
in Jesus' name.

331 In you, O God, we can be confident.
In you, O God, we can know trust.
In you, O God, we can find faith:
to renew our lives,
to restore our hope,
to confirm our call
to be what we are:
your children, brothers and sisters of Christ,
pilgrims together in truth,
seekers of peace,
questers for justice.
We approach you now in worship,
and pray we know you to be near,
here and now,
in all places and always
in Jesus' name.

332 God of mercy, forgive our sin.
You free us to be followers of Jesus,
but too often we chain ourselves to other ways
    and forget our calling;
too often we destroy the peace you give,
    by unthinking and uncaring acts;
too often we spurn the love you show
    and deny love to others;
too often we fall silent before injustice
    and compromise ideals;
too often we want to be Lord of all our days
    and reject the sacrifice of will and life.
Forgive us, we pray,
in the name of Jesus, Christ our Lord.

333 God of love and mercy,
we rejoice that you are a touching God,
who kissed the earth in Christ,
and embraced humanity
declaring us precious,
calling us and drawing us, by your mercy,
into fellowship with you.

Forgive us for living
like those stumbling in darkness,
as though your hand was not on our shoulder.
Forgive us for betraying
the hope that is in us
as though we were beyond your reach.
Forgive us for compromising
the justice we should seek,
and disabling the peace we could make
as though you no longer cared for your creation.

Help us to be truly sorry for failing you,
and then truly happy to know
that your offer is forgiveness
and freedom to find fulfilment.
In Christ's name we pray.

334   Thank you, living God,
for the sure foundation of our faith:
built not on rules, but on life:
your life in your Son Jesus Christ.

We thank you
that your offer of love is unconditional:
not governed by chance,
but by the deep and broad grace
you have shown the world in Jesus.
We thank you
that your call is not only to a few but to all:
a call to repent, a call to believe.

We thank you
that choice and not chance
governs our discipleship:
the choice to say 'yes',
and become followers of the Way.
We thank you
that your offer is for life fulfilled
through service and self-giving:
losing our lives to find them.

We thank you
that your Kingdom
is not built on fickle and temporary whims,
but the firm foundation principles
of justice and righteousness.
We thank you
that our life with you
is not a lottery but a firm offer.

Living God, we choose the life you offer,
and ask for strength
to live by your invitation.

335 Lord, we pray in resurrection hope for your world.
We pray for the voice of conscience crying in the wilderness:
> for the lone voice speaking out in the babble of indifference and neglect;
> for the pressure groups exposing injustice;
> and for the Church speaking to a godless world.

We pray for refugees fleeing from violence, and having trouble finding a welcome;
> for those who have resettled, but still long for the land of their birth,
> for young people leaving home to seek security or love,
> for those ill-treated by their marriage-partner,
> and for children caught up in a cycle of abuse.

We pray for those whose morale is low:
> because life has become a cul-de-sac
> because of illness in themselves or loved ones;
> because of grief or bereavement;
> because of unemployment or lost opportunity.

We pray for your Church in its mission and service, and especially
> for those with dwindling numbers;
>> may your resurrection power give hope.
> for those who struggle to be the conscience of society as part of their witness;
>> may your resurrection power give courage.
> for this congregation as we witness to our town, and each generation;
>> may your resurrection power give faith.

Lord, though our prayers may be small and weak, may those for whom we have prayed hear your eternal Word:
> *'Nothing in all creation can separate us from the love of God*
> *in Christ Jesus our Lord.'*

(Romans 8.39)

336 God of justice and peace,
we rejoice that your Kingdom is upside-down,
where those caught in the grip of poverty, sadness and despair
can find themselves blessed.

We pray for this our own church, and your Church round the world, that in a world too often driven by the measures of material success, we learn again and fearlessly proclaim Kingdom values.

Bless those in poverty, whether of body, mind or spirit;
  bless them with hope, and bless us with just compassion.
Bless those in sadness;
  bless them with peace, and bless us with real concern.
Bless those in despair;
  bless them with purpose, and bless us with patient love.
God of justice and peace, build your upside-down Kingdom:
  frail and fractured hearts knowing wholeness;
  the impoverished, riches;
  the weak, strength;
  the comfortless, inner resources.
So may joy be made complete.

337 Gracious God, we pray for our Church:
  its councils and its congregations;
  its ministers and its members;
  its young and its old;
  its committed and its fringe.
You have called us to be a channel of grace
and a sign of hope,
in a world hungry to hear good news.

You give us the ministry of reconciliation
in a world where communities are still divided and reconciliation is distant;
where poverty mars the life of many,
prejudice still distorts,
nation stands against nation, and community against community.

Yet light shines even in those dark places.
We celebrate the breaking of barriers,
the pulling down of walls,
the making of contracts,
the hard work of politicians,
the handshake of a neighbour,
the smile of a child
and the prayers of the Church.

Reconciling God,
speak your word of peace
and bless those who work in your name.

338 Loving God,
bless our church.
Bless us in our acts of worship;
singing, praying, praising, listening:
hungering to hear your word;
thirsting to know your way;
eager to tell out your love
and longing to proclaim the gospel.

We pray we be a place of shared concern:
a community of reconciliation;
a source of strength and sustenance;
a signpost standing tall
to pilgrims on the way
and to those still searching.

We pray we be a haven of healing
in a bruising world:
taking time to tell the tales of hope
and listen to the stories of suffering and joy.

We pray we be:
slow to condemn and quick to affirm;
slow to reject and quick to embrace;
slow to neglect and quick to care;
slow to ignore and quick to welcome;
that through who and how we are,
we may be channels of your life-giving grace
for the world.

339 God of healing and peace,
in Christ you reconciled the world to yourself,
not counting our trespasses against us.
As new creations in Christ, may we go
to witness to your renewing love,
to overcome the barriers that divide,
to be ambassadors of your reconciling good news.

Remembrance Sunday

340 Gracious God,
we heard you even in the sea of disorder
and the darkness of the void,
    crying 'Light and Life become!';
    and all Creation was begun.   **We gather to praise.**

Redeeming God,
we heard you even in the sin of destruction
and the night-time of sadness,
    crying 'Enough! Here is my Son:
    love and a hope for the future!'   **We gather to praise.**

Inspiring God,
we heard you even in the silence of sorrow
and the anguish of pain,
    crying, 'If God be for us, who can be against us!'
                                                  We gather to praise.

341 Lord, you remember your promises and your people,
you keep the living and the dead in your love and care.
We confess that our remembering is selective and prudent:
    we well remember what gave us delight;
    we readily remember the things we agreed with;
    we eagerly remember all that fitted our point of view;
and even when we truly remember the past,
we fail to apply the lessons we learned to our present tasks.

We remember the brighter times of World War II:
when songs had tunes, and people pulled together.
    Help us not to forget the partings that made songs so poignant,
    or the distress that gave a common cause.

We remember those who were away, fighting,
and those on the home front, gardening and caring,
making ends meet, and keeping things going.
> Help us not forget those who died on some foreign field;
> those who coped with death in the rubble of their blitzed street;
> or the pain of families divided, children orphaned and partners bereaved.

We remember with thanks and pride sacrifices made
by our own people and our allies.
> Help us not forget the pain they also endured;
> the agony of ordinary people in the nations we knew as enemies;
> the desecration of fields and crops;
> the grief that has continued down the years.

We remember the daylight raids and long nights in the air-raid shelters,
the Holocaust and the concentration camps.
> Help us not forget the killing fields of Cambodia;
> the massacres in Rwanda;
> the hills of the Falklands;
> the deserts of the Gulf;
> the streets of Beirut, Jerusalem, Sarajevo and Belfast ...
> and the violence that still claims lives.

Lord, deliver us from the sentimentality that cripples action,
and the destructive remembering that crushes hope.
Help us to use memory as a resource for peace.
In the name of Jesus who dies and rises again.

342 In remembrance of those
throughout time, all over the world who have died in war,
> we pray urgently today
> that children, women and men
> may become makers of peace.

We pray for children growing up
in violent surroundings,
or thinking, talking and playing in warlike ways.
> God, give to your people a new challenge;
> new ways in which to test their strength –
> in sharing power and risking non-violence.

O God, we pray for:
a new awareness of the battlefield within us;
new ways of channelling aggressive instincts;
new thought-patterns, language and ideas;
a new appreciation of the world as one community;
new methods of dialogue and negotiation;
new attempts to befriend those different from ourselves;
new readiness to forgive and reconcile;
new visions, new love, new hope ...
and a new faith, that the peace that passes understanding
can reach out from within us to embrace the world.

343 Lord, with thankfulness we show our respect for the past,
and stand in hope for the future.
We give thanks for those who made sacrifices,
and the freedom for which they fought.
We give thanks for those who faithfully recall the horror of war,
and remind us of its great price.

We give thanks for pride and discipline,
and remember horror and panic.
We give thanks for heroism,
and remember orders blindly obeyed.
We give thanks for purpose, meaning and identity,
and remember devastating loss.
We give thanks for the making of life-long friends,
and remember the loss of a generation;
the loss of loved ones.

We give thanks for service offered and a sense of duty,
and remember those who had no choice in the matter.
We give thanks for lives given to save others,
and remember lives wasted for a few yards of no-man's land.
We remember the courage of those who faced bullet and shell
and the different courage of those whose conscience would not let them kill.

Lord, we give you thanks for your gift of life,
that gives hope even in the times of death,
and renews us to face the coming days,
through Jesus Christ who gave his life for us.

344 Lord, we give you thanks for visions of peace:
when swords shall be beaten into ploughshares,
and people will live at peace and unafraid;
when the river of life will flow from you,
lined by trees, whose leaves shall be for the healing of the nations;
when you will be in the midst of your people,
when all will know you;
and your law will be written on their hearts.

We thank you that we see this beginning in Jesus.
In him national divisions break down;
for there is no longer Jew or Greek.
In him social divisions break down;
for there is no longer slave or free.
In him the division between God and humanity is broken down,
for he is human and divine.

Father, we thank you that the reconciling begun in Christ does not ignore the struggles or pain of life, but works through them to bring renewal. We thank you that he came as one of us, shared our common life, died and rose again. We thank you that your Spirit assures us that from this new beginning, peace and justice will grow, until all creation is taken up in dynamic harmony with you.

345 Gracious God,
Lord of nations,
Saviour of people oppressed
and rescuer of communities crying out for deliverance,
we turn to you this day
in a spirit of thanksgiving and of penitence.

Victories belong to you,
for only you know what is truly filled with glory;
you alone understand what is truly worthy of celebration.

As we reflect on the times of war's ending:
the sense of accomplishment
and the feelings of joy that a devastating war was over,
we ask you to accept our humble thanks:
thanks for those who gave their lives and their deaths
in order that justice, freedom and integrity
might still be signs of your Kingdom;

thanks for individual acts of heroism
and living examples of community co-operation
which were signs of hope on days of confusion and pain;

thanks that finally the dark days
of Holocaust and hatred were over
and they could be buried deep, never to dawn again;

thanks for the new ties which have developed over recent years
and the increasing trust amongst European peoples.

Now let your people in all places
be committed to reconciliation and peace,
so that the seeds of national arrogance, intolerance, prejudice and fear,
which can so readily grow into the horror of war,
may never again be sown in our lands.

In all our nations
let there be victories over poverty and greed;
let there be victories over anger and bigotry;
let there be victories over pain and disease;
let there be victories over despair and apathy.
And may you, our God, reign for ever and ever,
and the kingdoms of this world become the places
where your victory is recognized.
Through Jesus Christ, our Lord.

346 Lord, your love has helped your people in all ages, strengthening and guiding, urging and inspiring; love that is present in the struggles of life, yet offers hope for the future.

Lord, your love has ached, confronted with Goliath and Genghis Khan, with the mud of Flanders and the smoke of Auschwitz. We ask for your love to be with us now as we ache with remembrance of past sorrow and distress.

We pray for places where homes are destroyed and lives are laid waste because of war. We pray for places where the land is unsafe and people are still being maimed as they reap the harvest of land-mines sown in past conflicts. We pray for people who have had to flee from their country because of the threat of violence. Lord our remembrance is witness to the failure of humanity to resolve conflict without violence and anguish.

And nearer home, we pray for homes and offices where emotional violence distorts relationships. We pray for your Church where disagreements and personality-clashes misdirect our energy. Lord may your love still the conflicts within us, calm the waves of panic from past mistakes, silencing the nagging doubts that condemn us, and so draw out our humanity and warmth.

Lord, you have walked this way before us. Your love ached at the unmarked grave of your Son. You bore his lonely death and bloody agony. And from it all you brought healing for broken hearts and hope for us all.

Silently, we pray for those who grieve ...
    for those who are despairing or distraught ...
    for those who have lost a purpose in life ...
    for those whose memories are a burden rather than delight ...
    for all who need our prayers.

'Praised be the God and Father of our Lord Jesus Christ! In his great mercy by the resurrection of Jesus Christ from the dead, he gave us new birth into a living hope.'

(1 Peter 1.3)

347 We pray for the Church, O God,
that it burn with the flame of the Spirit,
and not shrink from proclaiming you
as a God of judgement.

We pray for the world,
and yearn that instruments of war
be beaten into machines of peace and plenty,
and conflicts between nations
yield to peace.

We pray for the world,
that those who play fast and loose with justice,
who oppress and exploit and disregard
the feelings and rights of others
may turn again and seek wisdom and walk justly.
In Jesus' name.

348 Saving God:
May our eyes shine with the light of hope.
May our voices be steady with the authority of experience.
May we move expectantly into the future,
as the landscape of your Kingdom
emerges from the insecurity of our passing world.

349 God of justice and peace,
we commit ourselves to the gospel of Jesus Christ:
spelling hope to the downtrodden,
justice to the oppressed, and new life to all.

God of justice and peace,
we commit ourselves to the gospel of Jesus Christ:
a gospel not just about words and creeds,
but about loving deeds,
measured by the commitment of Christ.

God of justice and peace,
we commit ourselves afresh to the gospel of Jesus Christ.

Church Anniversary

350 God of our past,
seen in the stories of your people,
shown in the glory of the gospel,
known in the mystery of faith,
we adore you.

God of our present,
seen in the birth of new life,
shown in the thirst of pilgrims,
known in the rhythm of praise,
we adore you.

God of our future,
seen in the eyes of a child,
shown in the ties of communion,
known in the prize of assurance,
we adore you.
In Christ's name.

351 Eternal God,
mother and father you are to us, friend and companion through the years.
You look after us, so we trust you;
you know us so well, yet still love us, so we feel safe with you;
you are utterly trustworthy, so we rely on you;
you are God, eternally love, so we worship you.

352 Here we are, Father and God, meeting in church on this special day. Yet we cannot meet without the crowded years pressing in on us.

We remember many other times when we have offered praise and prayer. We give thanks that, within your sustaining power, the urgency of praise has never left us.

We recall that long before our time, your people joined in fellowship to sing and pray, receive bread and wine, share faith and love. We give thanks that we stand within the succession of faith.

Boldly we affirm that ours are not the final voices of praise. Already you are stirring the hearts of younger people; already children are reaching out to you in wondering love. We give thanks that they meet you now, and will in the future where you already live.

Here we are, Father and God, meeting in church on this special day. What has been, what is, and what is yet to be, unite in the eternal presence of Christ among his people.

353 God of all ages,
you have travelled with your people
through the years.
You have shared moments of joy
and times of despair.
Be with us now
as we, like those faithful believers who have gone before us
and those who will come after us,
join to praise your name.

354 Dear God, we meet in this place as others have before us;
its calm brings us into your presence,
the very walls are hallowed by the prayers of generations;
pulpit, Bible and table are symbols of your word to us.
Here, therefore,
we sense the mystery of your presence;
feel the glory which is yours alone;
and reach for that which is higher than ourselves.

And yet, dear God, in that honesty which your Spirit gives,
we acknowledge that the calm is false unless it stills our inner heart,
that gifts of pulpit, book and table mean little,
    until they seize our imagination,
    alter our wills to your purpose
    and change our ways for the better.
In this time of thanksgiving, humble us into true worship.

355 We know your perfect love but we are not your perfect people.
We come to say that we are sorry.
We have looked at other churches;
    and envied their buildings,
    their worship, their activities and their fellowship.
Forgive us.
Help us to walk in our own path and be ourselves, as you would have us.

We have looked at other Christians
    and believed that because they are different, they are wrong.
Forgive us.
Help us to see the work of the Spirit in every church
and be prepared to learn from their experience of Christ.

We have not valued or used the gifts of everyone in the church,
and have prevented some from playing their part.
Forgive us.
Help us to become a community
where all feel welcome
and each one can contribute to the good of us all.

We have acted as though the future of the church
was more important than the coming of the Kingdom.
Forgive us.
Help us to share your priorities
and teach us to take risks in our church life.

We have planned our worship to make us feel good
rather than open ourselves to the awe-ful power
of your self-giving love.
Forgive us.
In all things, help us to become more Christlike.

356 As we celebrate another year together,
we offer God our thanks and praise:

For those whose vision led to the beginnings of this church,
   we praise and thank you, Lord.

For those whose faithful service maintained the Church's life and worship,
   we praise and thank you, Lord.

For all the worship which has been offered in this place,
   we praise and thank you, Lord.

For every activity which has helped faith to grow,
   we praise and thank you, Lord.

For all the love which has been shown in words and actions,
   we praise and thank you, Lord.

For moments of glory flashing through the routine of church life,
   we praise and thank you, Lord.

For all that we mean to each other and to you,
   we praise and thank you, Lord.

357 Eternal God, we proclaim with joy that Jesus Christ
is the head of the Church:
his life and death give meaning and purpose to our lives.
Give your strength to this church and to us as we serve it:
   may the teaching of Jesus be our guide;
   may the compassion of Jesus show us the meaning of love;
   may the sensitivity of Jesus help create our relationships;
   may the healing of Jesus ease our tensions;
   may the suffering of Jesus bring reconciliation in division;
   may the death of Jesus remind us of the cost of true discipleship;
   and may the resurrection of Jesus give us undying hope.

358 Prayer for the opening of a new church building

Visionary God, in whose heart the passion for community burned before time began, we thank you for those whose vision and commitment inspired the birth of this community *(number)* years ago. Today, in another new chapter of our history, we thank you for friends whose hope and longing has finally led us to this place – remembering particularly those who died before the vision was realized. We praise you that they live on within your household of saints, where no yearning withers and no dream dies.

Architect God, in whose mind each detail of the world was evolved, we thank you for those whose imagining and planning has guided this community's life through the ages, and whose fidelity has kept us true to Christ. Especially we praise you today for those whose wider view and clear-sightedness enabled your people to withstand disappointment, smile at frustration, and continue to move forward in faith.

Builder God, in whose hands the world is shaped, we thank you for those whose practical loving helps humanity to be human and the Church to be Christlike. For those who have placed themselves in Christ's hands to be living stones, whose quality of caring cements relationships within and beyond the Church, and whose praying lifts us out of cloistered concerns, we give you thanks.

Artist God, in the labouring of whose soul the earth is decked with beauty, we thank you for those who develop the talents you give them to make the world and the Church more lovely arenas for your activity. Today we thank you especially for the creativity and craftsmanship that have helped to furnish this sanctuary, to lift our spirits towards your Spirit and to signal the beauty of holiness.

God of tomorrow, we are glad that we cannot contain you within the walls of our yesterdays nor of this today. You break out both of our buildings and of our expectations. You challenge us to follow Christ into the unknown, to walk alongside the poor and suffering, and there also to find that we tread on holy ground. Thank you for surprising us with your free Spirit into new attention and new action.

We offer all our thanks and praises in the name and through the grace of Jesus Christ.

359 God of the ages and of today, celebrating our anniversary, we pray for the whole Church, throughout the world. We pray for:

> churches rejoicing in new members, and those anxious as numbers fall;
> churches well thought of by everyone, and those persecuted for their faith;
> churches rich in physical resources, and those poor in everything but spirit;
> churches in distant villages and towns, and those in our neighbourhood.

We pray for all who struggle to follow Jesus in the Church:

> those who want to belong, but are not made welcome;
> those who want to offer their talents, but are prevented;
> those who want to speak, but are kept silent;
> those who are rich in gifts, but not allowed to give.

In celebrating another year,
we look forward to what we can become
in the knowledge of what God has already done.

360 Lord, when conviction comes to us,
Each one, alone,
Within our solitude,
Then, help us listen to each other
And test our strong assurance
In the fellowship of Christian friends.

Lord, when conviction seizes a group,
And we agree;
Unanimously it seems,
No one against
And no abstentions,
Help us then to pause,
Listening for the faltering question
On the lips of silent ones,
To judge again just where
The Spirit truly speaks.

Lord, when tradition speaks out
Loud and clear,
And we are sure just what our fathers said,
And where our mothers' strong convictions lay,
Help us to set this given evidence
Against our present time with all its hopes
And your eternal Word of Life
That ever speaks anew.

361 Trusting and trusted God,
  in response to your unfailing love throughout the year,
  in response to your total commitment to us,
  what can we do?

We will give you our best, not our second best.
We will give you our heart, and not be half-hearted.
We will give you our time, not our spare time.
We will give you ourselves to become your people.

362 Eternal Lord of heaven and earth, your truth stands supreme:
    powerful in the lives of men and women;
    persuasive in its appeal to young people;
    kindling the love of little children,
    and reaching to the ends of the earth.
  Though cruel men attack it and fools ignore it;
  though we neglect it and friends deny it;
  even if the earth crumbles, the sky darkens and our hearts are full of fear;
  though people stop their ears, and messengers forget their task,
  still your truth prevails,
  waiting for the new time of its revelation.
  This anniversary day we affirm our confidence in you.
  Fit us to receive your truth.

363 Like a city on a hill,
    may your people's life be seen.
  Like a light within a house,
    may your people scatter darkness.
  Like a house on firm foundations,
    may your people be strong and secure.
  Like a church with open doors,
    may your people show their friendship.

The following people have contributed to this collection of prayers.

Stephen Brown is a minister in the United Reformed Church and currently serves a local church in Gatley, Cheshire. Prior to ordination, he worked in the computer industry. He writes, records and performs songs reflecting the Christian faith, in both the folk and rock idioms. He has a developing interest in the writing of both poetry and hymns.
He has written prayers numbered 1-3, 8, 10-13, 22, 24-26, 31, 33, 35-36, 39, 45, 46, 104, 106, 109, 111, 118, 119, 122, 123, 127, 128, 131, 134, 135, 137, 160, 161, 164, 165, 200, 201, 203, 204, 206, 207, 209, 210, 219-221, 330-334, 336-338, 340, 347, 319, 320.

Ann Buckroyd is Superintendent of the Huddersfield East Methodist Circuit. She has served five circuits, and for six years was Chaplain to the Methodist Conference 'Youth Makes Music, Dance and Drama'. She has a special interest in children's hymnody and was a member of the Text Committee for *Hymns and Psalms*. She has contributed to a number of books of prayers published by the West Yorkshire Methodist Synod.
She has written prayers numbered 51, 53, 56, 57, 60-63, 107, 110, 113, 115, 121, 125, 132*, 133, 140*, 224, 225, 227, 229, 267-269, 272. 273, 275. The prayers marked * first appeared in *This is our God* produced by the West Yorkshire Synod of the Methodist Church.

Kate Compston (URC, with Quaker leanings) enjoys writing, counselling, and leading retreats and workshops. She is committed to 'peace with justice for the whole of creation', likes walking, art, theatre, friends – and good chunks of solitude. Brought up on the Cornish coast, she now lives in Hampshire with her husband, daughter and labrador.
She has written prayers numbered 65-68, 69*, 70, 71*, 74, 75*,76*, 189, 191, 192, 195, 196, 198, 216, 236, 238, 240, 241, 245, 247, 385, 287, 289, 290#, 293, 342, 358. The prayers marked * first appeared in *Bread of Tomorrow* ed. Janet Morley, (SPCK/Christian Aid), and the prayer marked # in *Encounters* (URC)

Donald Hilton has compiled this collection. He is Moderator of the Yorkshire Province of the United Reformed Church. He has been minister in local churches in South Norwood, Gosport and Norwich, and for six years was Education Secretary of the Congregational Church. He is a regular contributor to the International Bible Reading Association and has compiled several anthologies including *Liturgy of Lifee* and other resources for Christian education and worship. He was co-editor of *Prayers for the Church Community* and editor of the *Living Worship* series.
He has written prayers numbered 14, 34, 54, 90, 103, 117, 141, 146, 151-156, 162, 167, 168, 171, 173, 205, 213, 215, 217, 231, 248, 270, 271, 274, 276, 278, 284, 295, 296, 299, 305, 351, 352, 354, 357, 360, 362, 363.

David Jenkins is Moderator of the Northern Province of the United Reformed Church. He has served pastorates in Leeds and Manchester, and held positions in theological training. He has contributed to numerous books of prayers and worship material including *More Every Day Prayers* and the *Living Worship* series (NCEC)
He has written prayers numbered 50, 52, 55, 58, 59, 64, 79, 81, 83, 86, 88, 93, 174, 177, 179, 180, 182, 185, 250, 252, 256, 258, 294, 297, 298, 300, 301, 345.

Kate McIlhagga, a graduate of St. Andrew's University, is a mother and grandmother, and a United Reformed Church minister in rural Northumberland with care of three churches. She has worked in youth and community development, as chaplain to a hospital and a theological college, and as a Community Minister in a church community centre. As a member of the Iona Community she is involved in issues of spirituality. She contributed to *Human Rites* and regularly writes for *All the Year Round* (CCBI).

She has written prayers numbered 9, 47-49, 72, 78, 82, 85, 89, 94, 97, 99, 159, 163, 166, 186, 187, 202, 208, 212, 214, 218, 222, 233, 242, 244, 283, 317, 320, 321, 323, 325, 327.

David Moore has worked as a Methodist Minister in Wales, London and Bradford. He is at present the City Centre Chaplain in Milton Keynes. Much of his work has been at, or beyond, the edge of the institutional Church. Dominating his interests is sculpture and he longs to carve wood all day!
He has written prayers numbered 77, 80, 84, 112, 120, 126, 136, 199, 211, 223, 226, 228, 230, 232, 235, 237, 239, 243, 246, 255, 277, 279-282.

Christine Odell is married to Peter Sheasby, and they live near Ilkley, West Yorkshire with their six-year-old daughter, Anna. Christine read theology at Lady Margaret Hall, Oxford, and is a Methodist local preacher. She has published a number of prayers and meditations, and a volume of prayers of intercession.
She has written prayers numbered 142, 147, 157, 169, 170, 172, 188, 190, 193, 194, 261, 263, 265, 302-304, 306, 307, 314.

Simon Oxley is Executive Secretary for Education for the World Council of Churches. He is a Baptist minister who has served in local churches and ecumenical appointments in the north west of England, and for eight years was General Secretary of the National Christian Education Council. He has written regularly for the International Bible Reading Association and for *Partners in Learning*.
He has written prayers numbered 87, 91, 92, 105, 129, 144, 148, 158, 262, 264, 266, 286, 288, 291, 292, 353, 355, 356, 359, 361.

Peter Sheasby is a Methodist Minister, trained at Hartley Victoria College, Manchester, and serving in the Ilkley Circuit. Married to Christine (Odell), his interests are worship and pastoral care. He has written and edited prayers for the Epworth Press and West Yorkshire Methodist District.
He has written prayers numbered 108, 114, 116, 124, 130, 138, 139, 176, 178, 181, 183, 184, 197, 249, 251, 253, 257, 259, 260, 308-313, 315, 316, 318, 319, 322, 324, 326.

Simon Walkling is minister of Christ Church United Reformed Church, Rhyl, which is his first pastorate. Before training he was a buyer for Lucas and was also involved in various aspects of church youth work. He seeks to blend traditional styles of worship with more activity-based and visual forms.
He has written prayers numbered 4-7, 15-21, 23, 27-30, 32, 37, 38, 40-44, 73, 95, 96, 98, 100 102, 143, 145, 149, 328, 329, 335, 339, 341, 343, 344, 346, 348.

Prayers numbered 175 and 254 were written by **Duncan L. Tuck**, a United Reformed Church Minister in Lowestoft.

Number	First line	Page

Index of First Lines

Part 1: The Christian Year

Advent

The Life of Jesus

Jesus: Healer, Teacher and Friend

Jesus: Lord and Servant

Mothering Sunday

Ascension, Pentecost, Trinity

Part 2: The Parallel Christian Year

Special Sundays
Bible Sunday

New Year

Week of Prayer for Christian Unity

Prayers for Christian Worship
Book 2

The Word
in
The World

Compiled by Donald Hilton and written by the same ecumenical team as *Seasons and Celebrations*.